"Pain is inevitable, but enduring it al[...] chelle Bengtson is a voice of hope who will speak into your struggles, a helping hand who will point you to Jesus, and a wise guide who will lead you through whatever you're facing so you can embrace more of what our good God has for you."

Holley Gerth, bestselling author of *What Your Mind Needs for Anxious Moments*

"Thousands of people suffer from daily pain. For some it is physical, and for others it may be spiritual or emotional. How do you maintain hope in the midst of chronic, unrelenting pain? *The Hem of His Garment* is an honest and transparent look at pain. Dr. Michelle Bengtson gives the reader permission to ask hard questions and practical guidance on how to seek God during times when you feel the most wounded. A beautiful gift for every person living with pain."

Dr. Saundra Dalton-Smith, physician, bestselling author, and host of the *I Choose My Best Life* podcast

"*The Hem of His Garment* sings hope in the minor key. It is an honest, profound, and deeply moving labor of love that will invite you to weep, worship, and pray. This book is a treasure for those who live in constant pain—and for those who long for a resource to give to friends and family who are hurting."

Carol Kent, founder of Speak Up Ministries, speaker, and author of *When I Lay My Isaac Down*

"Most people run away from pain, but Dr. Michelle Bengtson walks to it so she can walk us *through* it! While I was reading this power-packed and practical book, I was in extreme pain physically, emotionally, and spiritually, and Dr. Bengtson inspired me to pray, 'If I can reach the hem of his garment, Christ will touch the place of my pain with his presence, power, provision, and peace.' I will keep a stack of copies of *The Hem of His Garment* on hand as gifts for those who are feeling overwhelmed by the pain of life's storms."

Pam Farrel, author of *Discovering Hope in the Psalms* and bestselling *Men Are Like Waffles, Women Are Like Spaghetti*

"In *The Hem of His Garment*, Dr. Michelle Bengtson provides holistic, practical, and biblical strategies to help us move through our pain. Her approach to the seven different primary forms of pain, including the less commonly discussed emotional pain, relational pain, and secondary dynamics of pain inflicted by others, is a much-needed resource for faith-based medical and mental health professionals."

Michelle Nietert, MA, LPC-S, clinical director of Hope Helps, and author of *Loved and Cherished*

"*The Hem of His Garment* is a masterpiece of help and hope in deep pain. Michelle is the guide we all need when we've endured long past the timeline we gave God or when God seems silent despite our prayers. Sharing her journey of pain with raw vulnerability, Michelle shows us how to renew authentic hope and navigate suffering that seems too hard to handle."

Lisa Appelo, author of *Life Can Be Good Again*

"In *The Hem of His Garment*, Dr. Michelle well articulates walking through the journey of physical, emotional, relational, or spiritual pain. She guides us through solid biblical examples from Hannah to Job and how God walked with them through their painful journeys. Whether you are hurting from the past or in the midst of current pain, *The Hem of His Garment* will guide you to victory for his honor and glory."

Donna Fagerstrom, author, speaker, worship leader, and pastor's wife

"As a chronic pain sufferer and licensed therapist with comprehensive education on the subject, I have treated countless fellow pain suffers. I wish this book had been in my hands years ago because it would have been required reading for each patient and their loving family members. *The Hem of His Garment* by Dr. Michelle Bengtson is a true gift. It completely explores the annihilating effects of pain on our lives and on those of our loved ones. With biblical references and a myriad of suggestions, it also offers hope for the spiritual damage that aches to be healed. Bengtson nails it. For yourself or as a gift, and especially for someone newly diagnosed, this book is hope in your hands."

Deborah McCormick Maxey, PhD, licensed marriage and family therapist, licensed professional counselor, certified traumatologist

"*Through* is one of the most important words in my Life Coach Dictionary. Daily, I walk my clients to what I call 'the Threshold of Through,' where they must make the difficult decision to move from one side of their problem or issue to the other. In *The Hem of His Garment*, I now have a comprehensive and compassionate resource to place in the hands of my clients. Because Dr. Michelle Bengtson has stood at her very own Threshold of Through as a doctor, a wife, and a weary sojourner, she understands in a way that perhaps no one else could. Every page is tear-stained, truth-filled, and, most importantly, time-tested. I believe *The Hem of His Garment* will be a classic for generations to come."

Janell Rardon, MA, author, and trauma-informed board-certified life coach (AACC)

"Dr. Michelle Bengtson links her arms with yours and guides you through your journey with pain, whether it be physical, emotional, relational, spiritual, or something else. She reveals the deeper lessons of beauty she herself gleaned in the midst of her own painful experiences. With her help, you'll discover a deeper level of God's presence as you learn to overcome."

Linda Evans Shepherd, bestselling author of *Praying through Every Emotion* and *Make Time for Joy*

"*The Hem of His Garment* is an unapologetic call to action amid suffering combined with a deep dose of grace for those who are encumbered by trials. Dr. Michelle Bengtson is not a white-coat diagnostician but a chemo-chair sufferer who has endured each kind of pain she addresses. This book is honest, relatable, and practical—a weapon in the arsenal of anyone enduring pain!"

Tera Bradham DeNeui, Founder of the Heal Ministry and author of *Swimming for Freedom*

"Pain. There's no getting around it; we're all going to experience it. Dr. Bengtson gets that. She's been there too. With its sweet transparency and beautiful, relatable vulnerability, her biblical take on pain is refreshing. Physical, emotional, relational, spiritual, financial—all the pains. *The Hem of His Garment* offers the wisdom we need, the truth to help, and a gracious hand to hold. Exactly what we need to get through any kind of pain, as well as to offer support to those we love who are enduring pain."

Rhonda Rhea, TV personality, award-winning author of more than twenty books

"Ongoing physical, financial, and emotional challenges can be difficult to reconcile with the goodness of God. But *The Hem of His Garment* manages to hold space for these hard feelings while also steadying your journey. Dr. Bengtson extends an offer of liberation from the doubt and uncertainty that can come from prolonged suffering. Her brave choice to share vulnerable and uplifting stories made me feel understood on a deep level. With a desire to genuinely help, Dr. Bengtson leads us through a mindset recalibration. We learn to trade our guilt, impatience, and discouragement for God's love, grace, and power."

Jo Ann Fore, personal growth mentor and author of *When a Woman Finds Her Voice*

"Dr. Michelle Bengtson eloquently takes us on a journey grounded in biblical principles through the different types of pain and the consequences of it in our lives. She pulls back the curtain on our common misperceptions of pain's purpose and points us to hope in Jesus, the 'man of sorrows.' Dr. Bengtson's up-close relationship with pain gives weight to her words of encouragement to remain steadfast and focused on the Lord. Her chapter on lament is especially powerful, as she gives us a way to reframe complaints into life-giving lamentations. Journey with her 'through a valley of suffering, onto a ridge of faith, down a road of hopeful petition, and up to a peak of praise.'"

Jessica Van Roekel, author of *Reframing Rejection*

"Dr. Michelle's courage, compassion, and faith fill every page of *The Hem of His Garment*. As a fellow pain sufferer, I've cried out, 'God, can't you give me a how-to guide?' God has answered this prayer for those who are walking through the valley of pain. Drawing from the experience of her own suffering combined with biblical truths, Dr. B provides a step-by-step guide on how to walk through the darkness of pain yet radiate the glory of God. This book addresses the tough questions many silent sufferers want to ask but rarely discuss with others. Readers will find encouragement, support, and the inspiration to carry on amid their pain."

Shonda Whitworth, author of *Appeal to the Courtroom of Heaven* and cofounder of Fortress of Hope Ministries, Inc. (fortressofhopeministries.com)

"Today's world offers instant yet temporary, destructive, and addictive coping mechanisms for pain, making God's healing balm seem out of reach. Dr. Michelle Bengtson shines a vital light on God's timeless truths, giving us real hope in our valleys of despair to walk with God instead of away from his care. Readers find inspiration as they discover that *The Hem of His Garment* is not yesterday's miracle but today's truth to carry us through any storm."

Aliene Thompson, president of Treasured Ministries International

"I truly believe *The Hem of His Garment* is a book for everyone. Even if we haven't yet experienced debilitating physical pain, we've surely encountered emotional, mental, relational, financial, or spiritual pain, and we are surrounded by those fighting these difficult battles. Dr. Michelle Bengtson has packed this volume with comfort, encouragement, ministry opportunities, and even the path to spiritual healing. It's delivered with transparency and truth, built on a foundation of Scripture that encourages the reader to hold on when they want to give up. She gives us a precious gift—a hand to hold, permission to acknowledge the struggle, and the wisdom for coming alongside one another."

Edie Melson, award-winning author and director of the Blue Ridge Mountains Christian Writers Conference

"Fresh. Unpretentious. Honest to the core. In *The Hem of His Garment*, Dr. Bengtson addresses the hard and often ignored questions that engulf pain-filled seasons. Emotionally captivating and thought-provoking, this book is healing wrapped in print form. It will be an anchor to your soul and wings to your hopes. Join thousands of other readers who are discovering the silver lining when life does not seem fair or isn't making sense."

Tracey Mitchell, international speaker
and award-winning author

"As a fellow chronic-pain warrior, I very much related to the experiences Dr. Bengtson shared in *The Hem of His Garment*. Her book helped me feel less alone while offering practical strategies to persevere through circumstances beyond my control. The 'Hem of His Garment' passages at the end of each chapter particularly resonated with me by providing promises to cling to while I wait for healing. I highly recommend this book. By the time you finish it, you will have greater hope, peace, and a newfound perspective on pain that will usher you into a deeper relationship with God and others. I can't wait to give this book to the pain sojourners in my life!"

Jen Roland, writer, speaker, board-certified mental health
coach, and women's ministry leader

THE HEM
OF HIS
GARMENT

Other Books by Dr. Michelle Bengtson

Hope Prevails: Insights from a Doctor's Personal Journey through Depression

Breaking Anxiety's Grip: How to Reclaim the Peace God Promises

Today Is Going to Be a Good Day: 90 Promises from God to Start Your Day Off Right

THE HEM
OF HIS
GARMENT

*Reaching Out to God
When Pain Overwhelms*

DR. MICHELLE
BENGTSON

Revell

a division of Baker Publishing Group
Grand Rapids, Michigan

Published by Revell
a division of Baker Publishing Group
Grand Rapids, Michigan
www.revellbooks.com

Printed in the United States of America

Library of Congress Cataloging-in-Publication Data
Names: Bengtson, Michelle, author.
Title: The hem of his garment : reaching out to God when pain overwhelms / Dr. Michelle Bengtson.
Description: Grand Rapids, Michigan : Revell, a division of Baker Publishing Group, [2023] | Includes bibliographical references.
Identifiers: LCCN 2022037726 | ISBN 9780800742355 (paperback) | ISBN 9780800743079 (casebound) | ISBN 9781493441235 (ebook)
Subjects: LCSH: Pain—Religious aspects—Christianity. | Suffering—Religious aspects—Christianity. | Prayer—Christianity. | Healing—Religious aspects—Christianity.
Classification: LCC BV4909 .B467 2023 | DDC 248.8/6—dc23/eng/20230217
LC record available at https://lccn.loc.gov/2022037726

23 24 25 26 27 28 29   7 6 5 4 3 2 1

This book was forged through the crucible of pain,
and is dedicated to all my fellow pain sufferers,
because you understand,
but also because you need to know
someone understands you.

Contents

A woman who had a flow of blood for twelve years came from behind and touched the hem of His garment. For she said to herself, "If only I may touch His garment, I shall be made well."

Matthew 9:20–21 NKJV

They sent out into all that surrounding region, brought to Him all who were sick, and begged Him that they might only touch the hem of His garment. And as many as touched it were made perfectly well.

Matthew 14:35–36 NKJV

Let Me Link Arms with You

Dear Fellow Pain Sojourner,

I wept in pain through the night and early this morning, praying not only for my own healing from pain but also for the physical, emotional, spiritual, relational, and financial healing of so many I know and love, as well as for you, dear reader.

Years of enduring different types of pain have humbled me and made me grateful for the pain Christ experienced on our behalf. He paid for our sickness, our sin, our brokenness, our imperfection, and our pain knowing we could never truly appreciate it this side of heaven.

I want you to know that you will experience victory on the other side of your pain journey and that your victories are worth fighting for, but you don't fight alone. I have experienced each type of pain mentioned in the following pages. I come to you not as one who no longer suffers but rather as someone who knows the loneliness that accompanies the journey through pain and offers to link arms with you so you will feel less alone.

In our own strength, we may feel weak. But our faith is in a very strong God. It is my prayer that as you read through these pages, you will grow through the pain you go through. Hope lets us get up and face each day, pain-ridden as it may be, unsure of what it holds but confident in the One who holds it. Will you hold on to hope with me as we take this journey together?

God isn't just the God of heavenly thrones, churches, Bible studies, prayer meetings, and revivals; he's also the God of chemotherapy chairs, overdrawn bank accounts, prodigal children, empty chairs at holiday dinners, bathroom floors, broken hearts, and tear-stained pillows. He's a God who stoops and bends his ear to listen to our heartfelt cries. He's the God who promises to go before, walk alongside, and come behind when no one else will. I pray that as you read this book, you'll encounter him in a fresh new way through your pain and reach out to touch the hem of his garment.

Linking arms with you,
Dr. Michelle

1

Encouragement *through* Pain

About a year prior to the release of my first book, I was deathly ill, on medically prescribed bed rest, and being kept alive with IV hydration and nutrition. I plummeted from 113 pounds to a skeletal 74 and was so depressed from my isolation and confinement, I didn't want to go on that way. I had treated thousands of patients who had depression, and I recognized it in myself. I followed the advice I had given those patients for years: I rested, ate healthy once I was off the IV, slowly resumed exercise, and started therapy and medication. All those efforts helped, but I was disturbed to find that they weren't sufficient to eradicate the depression. As my depression continued, I looked enviously at others, those with energy and evident joy, and I began to believe I was joy-immune.

The longer I remained in that state, the more frustrated I became and the harder it was to keep fighting. I needed a reason to get up each day and face the world. That's when I learned the importance of encouraging myself in the Lord. A friend called the night before my scheduled surgery and lovingly reminded me of this truth: "Weeping may last through the night, but joy comes with the morning" (Ps. 30:5 NLT). To encourage myself, I crafted a very simple post on social media: "Today is going to be a good day because God's joy comes in the morning." A couple of weeks later, as I fought back depression's darkness, I wrote another post to encourage myself: "Today is going to be a good day because God's mercies are new every morning." Over time, this became a daily exercise for me that always started "Today is going to be a good day because . . ." and was based on one of God's promises. I left my posts open for public viewing, and they began to attract views and comments from others. Quite unintentionally, this turned into a six-year ministry of daily devotions about how and why we can experience a good day despite our feelings and circumstances when we trust in and stand on God's promises.

As I walk through my pain journey now, I am encouraged to see that what began as an encouragement for me turned into a book that has touched so many lives, Today Is Going to Be a Good Day: 90 Promises from God to Start Your Day Off Right.[1] *Especially on my highest pain days, I return to Scripture to encourage myself in the truth of the Lord. God brought me through those dreadful, pain-filled days, and I know he will do the same for you.*

A definition of *encourage* is "to inspire with courage, spirit, or hope."[2] When we're in the abyss of pain, our grip on the thread of truth may slip, and the temptation is to let go. Encouragement—or inspiration with courage, spirit, or hope—fortifies our grip and strengthens our resolve. Sometimes we must encourage ourselves, sometimes we need the encouragement of others, and always we need God's Spirit to encourage us to keep holding on, looking up, walking, waiting, and sometimes just breathing. We can be our own worst critic, and we must be careful what we say to ourselves because we are listening. Instead, we should consider speaking kind and grace-filled words to ourselves like we would to a friend. "Kind words are like honey—sweet to the soul and healthy for the body" (Prov. 16:24 NLT).

Encourage Yourself

In 1 Samuel, we read that David and several hundred of his men were away when a band of raiders from a neighboring region captured one of their hometowns, kidnapped women and children as slaves, looted the city, and burned it. Nothing remained of the city, their property, or their families when David and his army returned home. David and his men wept in grief, and his men talked of stoning him. When pain strikes our lives, our temptation is often to look for someone to blame.

In his grief and devastation, David likely had many questions, whether he voiced them or not. *If I'm a man after God's own heart, how could God let this happen to me? If I'm an anointed man of God, why must I hide from my attackers? Why doesn't God protect me?* David's situation is reminiscent of the situation Job found himself in; they both lost all they had, except God.

In his pain and discouragement, David had a choice, just as we do, to either blame God or encourage himself in the Lord and in what he *knew* to be true about God and his character. David offers us an appropriate model for our response to pain, suffering, and tragedy in our own lives. He reminded himself of the truths offered in Scripture and applied them to his situation: "And David was greatly distressed . . . but David encouraged himself in the LORD his God" (1 Sam. 30:6 KJV). Other translations say David "found strength" (ERV, NIV) or "strengthened himself" (ASV) in the Lord. Encouraging or strengthening

21

ourselves in the Lord requires intentionality. If we neglect this choice, we offer the enemy a blank canvas on which to write his lies and which stokes our natural impulse to cast blame on God. When pain ravages our lives and the enemy tempts us to become angry and blame God, we encourage ourselves by knowing, recalling, and affirming the truths of God's Word, especially those that rebut the enemy's lies.

> When pain ravages our lives and the enemy tempts us to become angry and blame God, we encourage ourselves by knowing, recalling, and affirming the truths of God's Word, especially those that rebut the enemy's lies.

When the doctor put me on bed rest and my spirit plummeted, I encouraged myself in the Lord by doing three things: (1) As I read the Word or listened to preaching or teaching online and came across Scripture that spoke to the pain of my heart, *I wrote the Scripture on sticky notes* and posted them on my IV pole, bedside lamp, bedroom door, closet door, light switch, bathroom mirror, car dashboard, and every other bare space. (2) Each time I saw one of those notes, *I read the Scripture out loud.* Scripture tells us, "So then faith comes by hearing, and hearing by the word of God" (Rom. 10:17 NKJV). Hearing God's Word out loud bolstered my faith and encouraged me. (3) *I repeated the verses several times* each time I saw them to help me remember them later.

Stones of Encouragement

In Joshua 3, God led the Israelites across the Jordan River, on dry land, into the promised land—a parallel to the miraculous Red Sea crossing they had experienced a generation before. Following the crossing, God called the people to pick stones from the riverbed, one for each of the twelve tribes, and create a monument on the riverbank to serve future generations as a physical reminder of God's faithfulness (see Josh. 4:2–9). Samuel used a similar stone of remembrance in 1 Samuel 7:12 to remind himself and others of God's faithfulness.

The stones themselves had no special power. They were simply tokens, visual reminders of God's past participation in their lives. We too can use stones of encouragement today to remind us of God's faithfulness. Consider keeping a written record of the instances when God demonstrated his participation or deliverance in your life. Or frame a photograph of a place where you were when you recognized that God met your need. I'm a simple girl: I like sticky notes with simple scribblings that encourage me to remember God's faithfulness. When my husband was diagnosed with a second form of cancer, I kept a sticky note on my mirror that said, "God healed him before, he can heal him again. Trust him."

Draw on Others' Encouragement

Sometimes in the depths of pain, we struggle to encourage ourselves. Sometimes the pain is so severe that thinking clearly is a challenge of its own. On those occasions, negativity pushes optimism aside, diminishing our ability to encourage ourselves. When this happens, we need external encouragement. First Thessalonians 5:11 reminds us, "Therefore encourage one another and build each other up, just as in fact you are doing." Pain promotes isolation and loneliness, yet God warns us in Genesis that he didn't create us to live alone. Our enemy wants to isolate us and cause us to question everything we know to be true about God and his character. All too often, that leads to a slippery slope into depression, discouragement, and despair. When you struggle to encourage yourself, after you've prayed

23

and shared your pain with the Lord, consider reaching out to a trusted friend, pastor, ministry leader, mentor, or counselor who will speak truth to you.

In the depths of my pain, I heard myself repeat Satan's lies. I *knew* they were lies, but at times, the weight of the pain made it difficult to rise above them. The pain swallowed me and left me in the darkest pit, like Jonah in the belly of the giant fish. In those times, I forced myself to reach out to a few trusted confidants. These are people I know I can be honest with about my pain, about my negative thoughts, and about my unanswered questions. I also know I can trust them not to varnish the truth and to speak it to me and over me. I don't always like it when they do (misery loves company, right?), but I am grateful because if they stooped to my way of thinking, then both of us would be sitting in the painful, hopeless darkness. Just knowing others are praying for me encourages me. Comfort comes when I know God has prompted others to pray. Please reach out to others who will encourage you, speak truth to you in love, and pray for you.

Go *through* the Storms of Life

We can consider pain a storm: We often have little forewarning of it, we feel trapped under it and miserable during it, and we have no inclination of how long it will last or how we will get through it.

> I've learned we are meant to go *through* the storms of life—not camp out there.

When was the last time you faced one of life's painful storms? Maybe you're there now. As I've pondered some of the recent storms of life, I've learned we are meant to go *through* the storms of life—not camp out there.

With the recent upheaval of the world, there's so much we don't know. So much misinformation, so many rumors, and for many, innumerable fears. We've missed worshiping in person together. We've experienced concerns for students, families, seniors, and businesses. In many ways, we've wanted to turn back the hands of time. But instead, God beckoned us his way—*through*.

> When you pass *through* the waters,
>   I will be with you;
> and when you pass *through* the rivers,
>   they will not sweep over you.
> When you walk *through* the fire,
>   you will not be burned;
>   the flames will not set you ablaze.
> For I am the LORD your God,
>   the Holy One of Israel, your Savior. (Isa. 43:2–3,
>   emphasis added)

Go through Grief

The year 2019 was a particularly painful one for me. I counted the passing of almost twenty friends and family members, mostly from cancer. No sooner would I find out about someone's new diagnosis than I'd hear of the death of someone else I loved, cared about, and had been praying for. I believed and still believe that God can and does heal, and yet my heart ached for the earthly losses of each of those who weren't healed this side of heaven but who now lived healed and whole in glory. Each new death seemed to compound the grief I already felt. I was comforted by Scripture and reminded that "Jesus wept" (John 11:35), so I knew he didn't condemn my grief but instead allowed it. Yet I also knew he didn't want me to stay in a permanent state of grief but rather journey *through* it with him.

His way is *through*.

> When you pass *through* the waters,
>   I will be with you. (v. 2, emphasis added)

Go through *Cancer*

My husband has received multiple different cancer diagnoses, and I've received a cancer diagnosis three times. Each time we've journeyed through cancer, we've reached for the hem of Jesus's garment and waited on his will and his way. God never intended for cancer to be a way of life, but he has allowed us to go through it and trust him to see us through it. There were so many times during each diagnosis and subsequent treatment when I thought for certain one or both of us might drown in the rivers of difficulty, and yet I knew God was in the rivers with us.

His way is *through*.

> When you pass *through* the rivers,
> they will not sweep over you. (v. 2, emphasis added)

Go through *Miscarriage*

"I'm so sorry. I can't find a heartbeat. We've lost the pregnancy." I sat stunned as the doctor delivered the words I could not have been more shocked to hear. The baby had kicked strongly the day before. And I had been giddy with excitement over making nursery plans and picking out baby names. This baby was a gift from God—until it wasn't. *How could this happen?* I wondered. I was healthy, and I had done everything "right." Grief suffocated me, leaving me unable to speak, and God allowed me to feel it for years afterward. Even though he didn't intend for me to stay there, I needed to go *through*.

His way is *through*.

> When you walk *through* the fire,
> you will not be burned;
>   the flames will not set you ablaze. (v. 2, emphasis added)

26

Go through *Depression*

After having treated thousands of patients in my career, no one was more surprised than I when I journeyed through my own valley of depression. I chronicled this journey in my first book, *Hope Prevails: Insights from a Doctor's Personal Journey through Depression*.[3] I'll never forget crying out to God in my despair and honestly sharing that if that was going to be my lot in life, I wasn't sure I wanted to continue living. Fortunately for me, God offered patience and gentleness as he revealed that a life of depression and despair was not his intention. Instead, he wanted to bring me *through* depression so I could share hope with others who suffered.

His way is *through*.

> Even though I walk
> *through* the darkest valley,
> I will fear no evil,
> for you are with me;
> your rod and your staff,
> they comfort me. (Ps. 23:4, emphasis added)

Go through *Job Loss*

I was puzzled when my husband walked through the door midmorning, a time when he was always at work. I had no words, just shock, as he explained, "I was laid off."

Wait . . . what? You lost your job? We had young children and a mortgage to pay! It took time to recover from the shock and recognize our own fears and anxieties. We didn't know what would come or where God would show up, but we came to trust that he would *see* us through it, but we had to *travel* through it.

His way is *through*.

27

One day Jesus said to his disciples, "Let us go over to the other side of the lake." So they got into a boat and set out. As they sailed, he fell asleep. A squall came down on the lake, so that the boat was being swamped, and they were in great danger.

The disciples went and woke him, saying, "Master, Master, we're going to drown!"

He got up and rebuked the wind and the raging waters; the storm subsided, and all was calm. "Where is your faith?" he asked his disciples.

In fear and amazement they asked one another, "Who is this? He commands even the winds and the water, and they obey him." (Luke 8:22–25)

Friend, pain presents various obstacles, but rest assured, God's way is *through*. Your current pain-filled landscape is not your destination.

Encouraging Lessons

As our family has journeyed through many of life's painful storms, I've learned a few things:

1. **We are meant to go *through* the storms of life—not camp out there. His way is *through*** (see Isa. 43:2–3).

2. **We must hold on to God's hand and his promises when the storms of life arise.** "For I am the LORD your God who takes hold of your right hand and says to you, Do not fear; I will help you" (Isa. 41:13).

3. **Even when we go through the storms of life, God never leaves us to go through them alone.** He promises to be with us anywhere we go and that he will never leave us or abandon us (see Gen. 28:15; Josh. 1:5).

4. **Storms may bring pain, doubt, or discouragement, yet he offers to be our comforter *through* the storms.** "Even though I walk through the darkest valley, I will fear no evil, for you are with me; your rod and your staff, they comfort me" (Ps. 23:4).

5. **We don't need to have the map; we just need to turn to the One who does.** When Jesus told the disciples, "Let us go over to the other side of the lake," he knew they would get there, but they forgot that promise when the storm arose (see Luke 8:22–25). God knows his plans for our life before they happen, and he goes through life's storms with us, taking us to the other side.

6. **We all experience storms in life, but when we look back, we can see God has gotten us *through* those storms each time.** "Be strong and courageous, and do the work. Do not be afraid or discouraged, for the LORD God, my God, is with you. He will not fail you or forsake you until all the work for the service of the temple of the LORD is finished" (1 Chron. 28:20).

In walking through my own pain journey and researching for this book, I've found a special affinity for the woman with the issue of blood in Scripture (see Luke 8:43–48). We'll discuss her experience in upcoming chapters, but I am most encouraged by her determination to reach out to touch the hem of Jesus's garment in faith, knowing that if she could but touch a tassel, she would be healed. Scripture assures us of the promise, "You know with all your heart and soul that not one of all the good promises the LORD your God gave you has failed. Every promise has been fulfilled; not one has failed" (Josh. 23:14). Because of this truth and because that woman is an inspiration to me, I close each chapter with a "Hem of His Garment" passage: a promise that we can cling to *while we wait* for the healing we know God can do. As you continue to read, I encourage you to make your own list of godly "hems" to hold in your heart as you put your trust in him.

As a neuropsychologist, I've also concluded each chapter with a "doctor's prescription" ("Your Rx"), to complete on your own to help you apply the material covered in the chapter. Sometimes I offer questions for you to ask yourself or God. Other times, points to ponder or consider in your own pain journey. Often I suggest pertinent Scripture to remember and hold on to when pain clouds your perspective. Just like any other doctor offering a prescription, I won't know if you follow the prescription. But I suspect you've opened this book and begun reading because you're tired of the pain you're enduring and are ready for a change. I want to walk this journey with you, believing that one day you'll be able to do that for someone else.

When I was so ill, on bed rest, and in great physical, emotional, and spiritual pain, I struggled to have the desire to praise God. During that time, however, I played praise and worship music 24/7 in my room. I discovered that even when I didn't *feel* like praising God, as the music played, I couldn't help but hum or sing along in praise. Scripture tells us that God inhabits the praises of his people (see Ps. 22:3 KJV), and I sensed his presence in that room. I also know that the enemy can't stand it when we praise God, and I love to infuriate the enemy. So, I've included a recommended playlist of songs at the end of each chapter to encourage you in your pain. The entire playlist can be found at https://drmichellebengtson.com/resources/playlists/.

It is my sincere prayer that this chapter will encourage you as you walk through your own pain journey. I also pray that

30

as you continue reading, you'll sense (1) a hand to hold as we look at the different types of pain (not just physical), (2) God's presence in your pain, (3) new perspectives on pain you may not have previously considered, and (4) some suggestions from both my clinical experience as a doctor and my personal experience as a fellow pain sojourner regarding what not to do as well as what to do to help mitigate your pain experience.

The Hem of His Garment

My comfort in my suffering is this:
Your promise preserves my life.

Psalm 119:50

Your Rx

1. From the suggestions in this chapter to encourage yourself, to construct stones of encouragement, and to draw on others' encouragement, which is most challenging for you and why? Prayerfully ask God to strengthen your ability to exercise that.

2. As you reflect on your pain journey, where do you find that you have become stuck? Prayerfully ask God how to move *through* it.

3. Which of the lessons mentioned above most resonate with you in your own pain journey and why?

4. Look up Psalm 23:4; Isaiah 41:13; and 1 Chronicles 28:20. Write the verses on index cards and place them where you will see them frequently. Read these passages aloud three times daily, committing them to memory. Ask God to reveal himself to you in your pain.

My Prayer for You

Father, what a privilege it is to pray for this dear one whom you love and know by name. I am comforted to consider that you know not only when they rise and when they rest but also the sources of their pain. When pain strikes and is all they can sense, help them to look to you and remember that you are with them, that you guide them, and that you will not leave or fail them. Help them to hold fast to your hand as you take them through *their painful trials to the other side. You have always been faithful before, so help them to choose to trust your faithfulness in this present suffering and in any future trial. Help them to encourage themselves in you. In Jesus's name, amen.*

Recommended Playlist

"Roses," Andrew Ripp, © 2021 by Andrew Ripp Music

"The Healing," Blanca and Dante Bowe, © 2022 by CURB|Word

"Shattered," Blanca, © 2020 by CURB|Word

"Healing God," Eleventh Hour Worship, © 2019 by Eleventh Hour Worship

2

What Is Pain?

"Describe your pain to me . . . What does it feel like? Is it sharp or dull? Stabbing? Aching? Throbbing? Is it constant or intermittent?" the doctor asked.

The questions were natural and expected, but I couldn't answer intelligently. All of the above and none of it at the same time, *I thought. As I considered his probing questions, my mind offered a multitude of other answers: raging, searing, shooting, burning, agonizing, torturous, tormenting, oppressive, wretched, and all-out miserable. How could I explain that it felt deeper than his stethoscope could hear and reached through my physiology to my mind and heart? How does one describe a pain that is all-encompassing and yet invisible to the naked eye?*

The Problem with Pain

We experience pain, endure it, attempt to treat it, and yet it's invisible. That's the problem with pain. Because no one can see what we endure, it's discounted. We can walk into a room, smile, and comment on the weather, and our pain goes unnoticed. If it does come up in conversation, it is frequently treated with averted eyes, a simple platitude, or the overly detailed story of another's experience.

So much of the suffering that accompanies pain is the simultaneous longing for immediate relief and the concern that things will never change. Through the pages of this book, we will take the pain journey together. We'll look at what pain is, what it does to us, some different ways to think about it or look at it, and how to fold our experience of pain into our relationship with our heavenly Father.

If you aren't going through a painful time right now, you either just came out of one or are preparing to enter one. It's not a matter of *if* but *when*. I'm coming to you from the valley of pain and suffering. I've written books from the far side of other painful experiences, such as depression and anxiety, with wisdom gleaned from the valley. This is different . . . I'm still enduring the pain and offering you a hand to hold amid *your* pain, along with the encouragement that you aren't alone.

Merriam-Webster defines *pain* as

1a(1): a localized or generalized unpleasant bodily sensation or complex of sensations that causes mild to severe physical discomfort and emotional distress and typically results from bodily disorder (such as injury or disease)

(2): a basic bodily sensation that is induced by a noxious stimulus, is received by naked nerve endings, is associated with actual or potential tissue damage, is characterized by physical discomfort (such as pricking, throbbing, or aching), and typically leads to evasive action

b: mental or emotional distress or suffering: GRIEF[1]

Pain and suffering coexist and are often referred to together, yet a subtle difference exists between them. *Suffering* is defined as "the bearing of pain, inconvenience, or loss; also, pain endured; distress, loss, or injury incurred."[2] It's a very fine distinction, but essentially pain is what we feel now whereas suffering is our ongoing experience because of today's event. Suffering includes pain. Pain is the discomfort, and suffering is the process of dealing with the discomfort, a sense of pervasiveness resulting from pain.

The suffering of both Hannah and Job is described as bitterness of the soul (see 1 Sam. 1:10 KJV; Job 10:1). Bitterness of the soul expresses suffering from the deepest part of us. Bitterness here is not the kind of negative emotion we experience toward someone else but rather something we experience viscerally that deeply indicates things are not as they should be.

In my decades as a neuropsychologist, patients' motivation for seeking help has been evident: the elimination of pain. Evaluating and treating patients enduring pain, suffering, and grief has taught me that each individual experience of pain varies widely based on multiple factors, such as our early life experiences, our basic personalities, our upbringing regarding how to cope with adversity, the depth of our relationships, and the degree of our acceptance of and faith in a sovereign God.

Types of Pain

Our vocabulary doesn't let us get a good grip on our pain. Even within the field of psychology, there is a dearth of commonly agreed upon definitions for the different types of pain. To name a thing provides some sense of control or understanding of it, but in our twenty-first-century, Western culture we lack the lexicon to adequately describe pain. This absence of appropriate descriptors diminishes pain's existence and makes it harder to manage. Our culture is largely dismissive of pain and insensitive to its sufferers because of this inability to describe it in addition to our reluctance to acknowledge and address negative topics in general.

For the purposes of this book, I've offered general definitions of the types of pain, recognizing that exhaustive definitions and explanations are nearly impossible for the reasons mentioned above. Physical pain is the most easily identified and understood. Yet physical pain is an incomplete representation of pain endured on this earth. Before we can move forward into addressing how we cope with pain, how others help or worsen our pain, where God is in our pain, and how we can develop a useful perspective on pain, we must explore pain in its variants.

Most of us have endured significant pain over the course of our lifetime, and we know pain when we experience it. How we relate to what we consider painful situations may differ entirely from how others experience them, yet that in no way minimizes our experience of pain. Pain equates to discomfort or distress caused by noxious or offending stimuli. It's an unpleasant experience ranging in severity from mildly annoying to excruciating and is indicative of some underlying condition or trigger.

The following may not be an exhaustive list of types of pain, but it covers those that are perhaps most readily recognized and that I've identified from a cursory review.

Physical Pain

Essentially, physical pain entails a feeling or perception of discomfort that is connected to an illness or injury in some part of the physical body, such as pain from a broken arm or a stomachache. Physical pain is perhaps the most easily understood because we've all stubbed a toe, had a headache, or worse.

Emotional Pain

Simply stated, emotional pain is discomfort or mental anguish caused by a negative, nonphysical origin but that continues to replay in our mind, resulting in mental or emotional distress. Emotional pain is the angst that is experienced with the myriad of negative emotions that cause us to question or downplay our value, worth, or identity. Prolonged emotional pain often precipitates discouragement, depression, anxiety, or despair and frequently leads to self-medicating behaviors such as drinking, reliance on drugs, overspending, and even workaholism at times. The lack of resolution of such feelings can result in chronic emotional pain that continues to play out in other circumstances or areas of life.

Spiritual Pain

Spiritual pain is perhaps one of the lesser discussed aspects of pain, at least with such a label, though many endure spiritual pain even if they don't define it that way. Spiritual pain here is considered a disruption in one's belief system or sense of relationship to God. Such pain, discomfort, or angst may accompany the times in our life when we feel like God has abandoned us, turned his back on us, punished us, or simply allowed instances into our life for which we see no redeeming quality. These perspectives cause us to feel uncomfortably distanced from God and distressed by that sense of distance.

Financial Pain

Financial pain often results when we lose the stability of an income or when we lose the ability to continue an accustomed standard of living. It can also be triggered by a financial loss significant enough that future goals or hopes are threatened. That loss can have far-reaching implications and contribute to other types of pain (e.g., emotional pain, spiritual pain, etc.), but the primary contributor is the situation that caused the financial loss or penalty.

Relational Pain

Relational pain often bleeds over into other kinds of pain, like emotional and physical, but it is essentially the pain and suffering that results from the breaking of or damage to significant relationships. We often experience relational pain secondary to betrayal, rejection, or abandonment. This pain calls us to question the true authenticity of a relationship, of others' motives, and of events that took place or words spoken. Some relationships die a slow death over time from a lack of contact or from lives moving in different directions, but relational pain often results from a sudden break in relationship ties that were perceived to be stronger than perhaps they truly were.

Grief

In its simplest form, grief is an acute pain and sorrow we experience with loss—the loss of physical functioning, the loss of emotional well-being, the loss of a relationship, or other losses. Grief is normal and natural and is involved in many experiences of pain. Grief is the bereavement and processing of the loss associated with pain, and it is attended by its own challenges.

Secondary Pain

Secondary pain is the painful experience caused by the words or actions of others, either intentional or unintentional, that worsens the pain we already fight. Frequently it comes in the form of blame or criticism, even if well intentioned:

- Friends, loved ones, or even strangers offering their opinions on what caused your physical condition, relationship difficulty, financial woes, perceived distance from God, or other unfortunate circumstance.

- Competitive-type comments from others about how their situation is worse than yours.
- Comments that minimize or shame the pain sufferer, such as "This too shall end," "Others have it worse than you," or "What doesn't kill you makes you stronger."

These comments that are offered as a panacea for our pain or as a glib dismissal are received in a way that makes the pain sufferer feel inept, incompetent, and guilty. It is likely that in the sufferer's efforts to diminish the pain, he or she has already considered the suggested cures and treatments offered by others. When others say or do nothing in an effort to avoid saying or doing the wrong thing, it can also cause secondary pain by making the one enduring pain feel unseen, unloved, and uncared for.

Pain poses a challenge to even the strongest of individuals because we often can't anticipate its onset, and its insidious nature leaves us longing for relief but not knowing how long the pain will last or how deep it will be. It can persist from day to day, week to week, and in many cases year to year with no clear end in sight. Pain tests our confidence in ourselves, our response to others, our trust in God, and our perseverance.

Pain tests our confidence in ourselves, our response to others, our trust in God, and our perseverance.

Another key factor that complicates pain is when one type of pain compounds another. Too often multiple types of pain are present simultaneously: emotional pain complicating physical pain, financial pain escalating grief, relational pain causing emotional pain, and so on. Healing becomes complicated since the resolution of one manifestation of pain may not bring resolution to the associated types of pain. The most tenacious of individuals are tested under such circumstances.

Role Models in Suffering

The Old Testament character Job provides a perfect model for working through pain because he experienced every type mentioned above, and simultaneously at that!

Ponder for a few moments that God considered Job blameless and of complete integrity, a man who feared God and avoided all evil (see Job 1:1). Right there I don't measure up. I mess up every day, and as important as integrity is to me, I have failed on numerous occasions in that department . . . but I digress. Not only was Job considered blameless and of complete integrity but he was also the richest person in the region (v. 3).

Despite accolades from God, a life well lived, and a full bank account, Job was not spared pain. God gave Satan permission to "do whatever you want with everything he possesses" (v. 12 NLT). Satan wasted no time. In short order Job lost all his children to a freak windstorm. He lost his livestock—his major asset and form of financial support—and suffered the deaths of his shepherds, servants, and farmhands. That alone would cause great pain for any of us, and it certainly brought on financial pain as well as grief for Job.

Job's story doesn't end there. He maintained his integrity despite those losses. Then Satan inflicted physical pain on Job with sores that covered his body (2:7). As if that wasn't enough, Mrs. Job couldn't relate to Job's perseverance or his acceptance of the fact that God allows both good and bad to befall his children. She brought conflict, and relational pain, into the relationship when she advised Job to "curse God and die" (v. 9).

For many of us, comfort comes through the presence and support of well-intentioned friends, though this is difficult for many who can't relate to our pain and don't know what to say or how to react. Job's friends initially supported him by coming to his side and sitting silently with him in his grief for seven days and nights (vv. 11–13). But then they began to opine on the reason for his pain and suffering, which consumes most of the book (chaps. 4–37). In their diatribes, Job's friends accused him of causing his own pain (which only makes pain worse and creates additional emotional and secondary pain). We find out later in the book that most of their opinions and advice were wrongheaded. But Job began to question his faith, his God, and the reasons God allowed his suffering (enter spiritual pain). Job's response to his pain and the lessons he gained therein have much to offer us, so we'll check back with him in future chapters.

Pain colors our perspective, robs us of the best parts of us, and challenges us to just barely cling to the hem of Jesus's garment. In the Gospel of Luke, we learn of another individual in need of physical healing. After twelve years of infirmity, the woman with the issue of blood knew she desperately needed physical healing. The story goes like this:

> As Jesus was on his way, the crowds almost crushed him. And a woman was there who had been subject to bleeding for twelve years, but no one could heal her. She came up behind him and touched the edge of his cloak, and immediately her bleeding stopped.
>
> "Who touched me?" Jesus asked.
>
> When they all denied it, Peter said, "Master, the people are crowding and pressing against you."

But Jesus said, "Someone touched me; I know that power has gone out from me."

Then the woman, seeing that she could not go unnoticed, came trembling and fell at his feet. In the presence of all the people, she told why she had touched him and how she had been instantly healed. Then he said to her, "Daughter, your faith has healed you. Go in peace." (8:42–48)

We can't know for certain, but it's reasonable to suspect that she dealt with each type of pain we've been discussing. Physical pain from her issue with blood. Financial pain because she had spent all her money on doctors and likely couldn't work in her physical condition. Emotional pain from the years of rejection and ridicule such a disorder promoted in those times. Relational pain resulting from others choosing to not associate with an unclean woman, likely leaving her single or divorced. Spiritual pain as a by-product of knowing God could heal but for whatever reason hadn't. Secondary pain from those around her accusing her of causing her own suffering, lacking in faith, or not trying their suggested remedies. And possibly grief not just from the loss of relationships or opportunities to provide for herself financially but also from the loss of hopes and dreams for her future.

> Pain colors our perspective, robs us of the best parts of us, and challenges us to just barely cling to the hem of Jesus's garment.

Despite her compounded pain, this woman did something awe-inspiring: She maintained her faith that if she could just *touch* the hem of Jesus's garment, she would be healed. I don't know what your areas of pain are, but I know that in the darkest nights of my pain, the enemy has tempted me to give up my faith in God. He has lied to me repeatedly and caused my heart to question the goodness and sovereignty of my heavenly Father. This woman suffered for over twelve years, and yet she maintained her faith and put it into action. It is my prayer that we will grow our faith as we walk this pain journey together.

The Hem of His Garment

"Because he loves me," says the LORD, "I will rescue
 him;
 I will protect him, for he acknowledges my name.
He will call on me, and I will answer him;
 I will be with him in trouble,
 I will deliver him and honor him.
With long life I will satisfy him
 and show him my salvation."

Psalm 91:14–16

Your Rx

1. Consider the different types of pain. Make a list of specific pain points under each type that you desire God to heal.
2. Consider Job, Job's wife, and the woman with the issue of blood. Whom do you most identify with and why?
3. Look up Psalm 91:14–16; Joshua 23:14; and Luke 8:48. Write the verses on index cards and place them where you will see them frequently. Read these passages aloud three times daily, committing them to memory. Ask God to reveal himself to you in your pain.

My Prayer for You

Father, you did not create us for pain in a perfect world, but you warned us we would experience painful trials in this life. Having faced so many painful circumstances in my own life, my heart goes out to the fellow pain sufferer holding this book in their hands. I thank you that we do not experience these pain-filled trials alone but that you go before us, you come behind us, and you hem us in on both sides. You are Jehovah Rapha, the God who heals, and Jehovah Jireh, the God who provides. I look to you to heal this dear one and provide for their every need on their pain-filled journey. In Jesus's name, amen.

Recommended Playlist

"Jireh," Chandler Moore and Naomi Raine, © 2021 by Elevation Worship Records

"Steady Me," Jeremy Camp, © 2021 by Stolen Pride Records, LLC

"From Everlasting (Psalm 90)," Sovereign Grace Music, © 2022 by Sovereign Grace Music

"Take This," Out of the Dust, © 2019 by Out of the Dust

3

Crawling from
Moment to Moment

Just recently, before my eyes even opened for the day, pain burned through my neck, up my scalp, down my shoulder blades, and into my collarbone like hot, smoldering coals in the middle of a campfire. "I can't do this," I lamented. Physically, the pain I endure has historically escalated throughout the day, from nonexistent or minimal in the morning to at times intolerable levels by the evening hours. So waking up in such a state didn't lend much hope for the day. Between book edits, emails, podcast episode preparations, and the normal tasks of daily life, deadlines loomed, yet I knew my inability to lift my head off the pillow threatened to sideline my day.

"But Lord," I beckoned. "How am I going to do what you've asked me to do when the pain renders me ineffective? How is this good for the kingdom or bringing you glory? Where is the Great Comforter when comfort eludes me?"

Perhaps the most frustrating aspect of the entire scenario was that I longed to hear God say, "I am with you, my child. I love you, sweet daughter. Let me do the heavy lifting." Or perhaps one of my heart's deepest desires: "Your faith has made you well." Yet I heard nothing. Nada. Zilch. For months on end. What does that say about me? What does that say about God? Where do we go when God seems silent yet the pain screams?

Surviving Pain in Faith

How does it make you feel if you project yourself five, ten, or twenty years into the future, in this same condition, when pain has stolen the best of you and you don't think you can continue in this state? I suspect that if we could converse with Job over a cup of java, he might admit to similar feelings. How did he feel as his friends berated him and God didn't come to his defense or his rescue? How many times did he cry out to God without a direct answer?

After Job lost all his livestock, servants, and children, Satan had another conversation with God intimating that being stricken with illness would make Job cave and curse God in his anguish. God allowed Satan to interfere with the one thing Job had left—his health—provided he didn't kill Job.

After Satan attacked Job's health, Job grieved his loss. He used a piece of broken pottery to scrape his skin while he sat among the ashes in his grief. Even today, people often cut themselves to numb the pain or to punish themselves or others. Job didn't minimize his pain or sweep it away with some popular cliché. He experienced the real and raw pain in a way that others observed. Yet in Job's account, we see how others tried to instruct him in how to cope or grieve even while Job was crawling from moment to moment just trying to survive.

46

Mrs. Job often gets a bad rap because she said to her husband, "Are you still trying to maintain your integrity? Curse God and die" (Job 2:9 NLT). Those comments may seem insensitive and cruel, yet we must remember that although she isn't mentioned much in Job's disastrous, painful experience, she too suffered greatly. I can't imagine being the mother who lost all ten of her children at one time. The grief of that alone could explain her resignation and her desire to blame God. What mother, having lost her children, wouldn't reasonably ask, "God, you could have prevented this. Why didn't you?"

She didn't just lose her children. She lost her financial provision. She lost the servants who helped her complete her daily work, which she then had to manage alone. And in an instant, she became a caregiver to her husband. While Job is the focus of the story, Mrs. Job also suffered immeasurable pain and likely felt as if she too was crawling from one moment to the next. Her grief is valid even if it was expressed differently or her faith was tested differently than her husband's.

Job's response to his wife attests to the man God considered blameless and of complete integrity: "'Should we accept only good things from the hand of God and never anything bad?' So in all this, Job said nothing wrong" (v. 10 NLT). Job was under no delusion that we only deserve good from God, and in faith he respected God's will and plan.

Where Pain Takes Us

When pain cripples us to the point of crawling from one moment to the next, in our humanity we're left wondering what that says about God. One of the clichés that bothers me most is "God never gives us more than we can handle." I've searched and haven't found that anywhere in my Bible. In fact, I've found that God allows us to endure more than we can humanly handle so we remain dependent on him. He wants to be the Lord of our life, which means we rely on him rather than try to negotiate life on our own terms and in our own strength.

> **God allows us to endure more than we can humanly handle so we remain dependent on him.**

It's one thing to endure pain with the hope of an end on the horizon. It's entirely different to endure pain in the absence of an explanation or path to resolution, as Job did. It is in that crucible that our faith is tested. As we crawl from moment to moment, barely holding on to our hopes and dreams of a pain-free future, our pain often drives us to confront our understanding of ourselves, our world, and God, of who he is and what part he plays in our lives. Pain adds an urgency that drives out the distractions and complacency that allowed us to avoid confronting these things before.

Pain prompts us to fall back on the coping mechanisms forged during previous trials throughout our life. Coping mechanisms are conscious or unconscious changes in behavior that we use in an effort to increase our sense of control in stressful situations and help us get through such trials as unscathed as possible. Some coping mechanisms are positive to our overall well-being, such as prioritizing rest, eating nutrient-rich foods to fuel our body, exercising to lower our cortisol levels, or calling a friend to pray. Unfortunately, some coping mechanisms may feel good in the moment but are detrimental to our overall well-being in the long run, such as sleeping too much, drinking to numb the pain, abusing prescription drugs or illegal substances, or spending money we don't have. The last thing a pain sufferer wants is one more thing to do, but it's important that we continually assess the short- and long-term benefits of those coping mechanisms we rely on to get us through pain.

Painful Trials Serve a Purpose

James 1:2–4 gives us great insight into how to reframe our focus when the pain is unending and we long to return to a pain-free existence: "Consider it pure joy, my brothers and sisters, whenever you face trials of many kinds, because you know that the testing of your faith produces perseverance. Let perseverance finish its work so that you may be mature and complete, not lacking anything."

I shared in *Hope Prevails* that when I was physically ill, on five months of medically prescribed bed rest, and in the valley of depression, I began to wonder if I was joy-immune because I tried all the usual recommendations I had given my patients over the years, including therapy, medication, diet, exercise, and rest, but they were not enough to eradicate the depression or let me experience joy.[1] The physical and emotional pain felt suffocating. It's easy to believe that James is commanding us to feel joyful in every situation. Yet he says to *consider* it joy—a verb, an action, rather than an emotion. In our painful journeys, God offers us the opportunity to contemplate the joy that can result when we confront our concept of ourselves, our world, and God *in light of God's Word*. James doesn't address the resolution of his readers' situations, but he emphasizes the blessing and personal satisfaction (joy) that come from candidly recognizing our own limitations, skewed perspectives and expectations, and weaknesses, including pain. He invites us to step out of the driver's seat and lean on our heavenly Father for wisdom, strength, peace, and God's own presence as we walk the path of pain.

Part of our learning process is realizing that painful trials serve a purpose: They test our faith. What do we believe about God and why? What do we believe about how God perceives us and relates to his children? In the testing of our faith, we develop perseverance, which is necessary as we progress toward our finish line in life. As we develop perseverance, we mature and become more like Christ.

I'm comforted that James's passage doesn't end there. While I long to become so like Christ that when others look at me, they really see his image in me, there's still so much I don't understand. Even in writing a book on pain after having endured each type of pain—sometimes multiple types simultaneously—there is still so much I don't know. But God doesn't chastise us for what we don't know. James beckons us to come to God with our doubts, fears, and questions and to ask for his wisdom. "If any of you lacks wisdom, you should ask God, who gives generously to all without finding fault, and it will be given to you" (v. 5).

I'm thoroughly convinced that if we never endured pain, we would develop a false sense of security that we know all we need to know and that we are capable of successfully managing our own lives without the influence of a loving or sovereign God. Not only does God not chastise us for asking him for wisdom, but he is a God of such abundance that he lavishes it upon us, knowing we need it.

James gives another wisdom-filled nugget to those of us who feel like we are crawling from one painful moment to another: "But when you ask, you must believe and not doubt, because the one who doubts is like a wave of the sea, blown and tossed by the wind. That person should not expect to receive anything from the Lord. Such a person is double-minded and unstable in all they do" (vv. 6–8). I've been guilty of knowing that God *can* heal and *does* heal, and I've prayed innumerable times for him to heal me, but in all honesty, some of those prayers have been wrapped in doubt. James reminds us to use our times of trial to expand our prayer life and to pray without doubting.

Do All to the Glory of God

I've had some very difficult days lately, pain-wise. The day after the release of my last book, *Today Is Going to Be a Good Day*, I felt like I had hit a wall. My bones were on fire before my eyes opened, hurtful conversations with someone close to me reverberated in my head, and secondary pain from those who blamed my pain on my schedule rather than empathizing with my state washed over me like a shame-laden wet blanket, leaving me unable to get out of bed for days. I had pushed hard through the book-launch season, yet I had tried to take care of myself, planning ahead to minimize additional demands and pacing myself. But it wasn't enough.

As tears streamed down my face out of frustration for all I could not do, lies flooded my mind: *You're not that old—you should be able to do more. You give up too easily—people are going to think you're lazy. God won't be proud of you when you complain about your pain and your inability to do things. With your increasing pain, you'll never be able to enjoy it when your children give you grandchildren.*

I felt like I crawled my way to the living room, where I found my husband diligently working on his Bible study preparation for the next day. "Are you busy?" I hesitantly asked him.

He then proceeded to share the insights he had gleaned from the particular passage he'd studied that morning. Meanwhile tears leaked from my eyes and made their way down my cheeks. "What's wrong, honey?" he asked.

For a moment, I sat speechless before asking him if we could talk. Over the next hour or so, I choked out a confession of the severe pain that engulfed my body, the overwhelming exhaustion yet sleeplessness over the past several months that had reminded me of my sleep-deprived newborn-parenting days from nearly two decades before, and the desperation I harbored when I considered the deadlines I faced in the coming few weeks.

His eyes glistened ever so slightly as he moved from his recliner to the spot right next to me. He reminded me of the lesson I seemed to have to relearn every so often: that my worth is not based on my productivity or met deadlines but by my position in God's family, saved and sealed by the blood of Jesus. He encouraged me to put my scheduled tasks aside for the day and give my body the much-needed rest it begged for. As I began to protest, he reminded me of John 4:6, in which Jesus, weary from his journey, rests at Jacob's well at midday. "If it's good enough for the Savior of the world," my husband teased, "it's good enough for the number-one new-release author of the week."

Sometimes it's hard to remember that our physical state doesn't minimize Jesus's mercy, goodness, power, and redemption; it accentuates it. My good days lull me into false self-dependence and a hope that God will be pleased with all I do for him, while my painful days—when I'm a hostage to my bed, unable to do much other than read my Bible and listen to praise and worship music—offer me a greater opportunity to practice gratitude for who God is rather than what he does for me. When God implores us in 1 Corinthians 10:31 to do everything to his glory, that includes the times when our best is lying in bed,

> **Sometimes it's hard to remember that our physical state doesn't minimize Jesus's mercy, goodness, power, and redemption; it accentuates it.**

resting our bodies. May our times of rest be holy acts of worship, covered in his mercy and grace.

Strength to Endure

I haven't always expressed the unwavering faith that Job did. These last couple of years have been a battle, physically, emotionally, relationally, and spiritually, for me and my family. Betrayal and relationship pain caused me to question what I thought was true about myself. Pain-filled, sleepless nights left me feeling weary and exhausted. One of the worst things about being strong is that nobody knows when you're in pain and hurting. Somehow the invisible pain we suffer can seem like the worst of all pain. If I had a dollar for every time I've heard "You look great!" when I was feeling anything but great, I could fund a hefty chocolate and coffee habit.

But in God's goodness, graciousness, and mercy, he led me to a verse that I *know* I have read every time I have read through the Bible, yet it was as if I had never seen it before, and it was just what I needed: "But you will not even need to fight. Take your positions; then stand still and watch the LORD's victory. He is with you. . . . Do not be afraid or discouraged. Go out against them tomorrow, for the LORD is with you!" (2 Chron. 20:17 NLT).

Do you ever wonder if you are strong enough to endure what you're going through? Strong enough to make it through? Strong enough to pass the test? You are. Because it's not up to you. It's up to God. In all our trials and pain, we have access to the God who is present and who provides. He wants us to know him, and he drives our attention toward him, but he also offers his presence with us and his wisdom, strength, peace, and, unbelievably, even his joy.

53

I don't know where you are or what painful battle you fight right now, but God says you don't need to fight. Fighting is exhausting and leaves us battle-weary. Wait on his victory on your behalf. He is with you just as he was with Job.

The Hem of His Garment

He gives strength to the weary,
And to the one who lacks might He increases power.
Though youths grow weary and tired,
And vigorous young men stumble badly,
Yet those who wait for the LORD
Will gain new strength;
They will mount up with wings like eagles,
They will run and not get tired,
They will walk and not become weary.

Isaiah 40:29–31 NASB

Your Rx

1. Pray and ask God to remind you of your response to the onset of your pain. If it was less than complete trust in God's ability to bring good from your experience, repent and ask God to increase your trust in him.

2. In the hours (or days or weeks) when you feel like you are crawling from moment to moment, barely hanging on, reflect on how God has strengthened you in the past, and record it in a journal you can look back on when your trust wavers.

3. Look up Job 2:10; James 1:2–8; and Isaiah 40:29–31. Write the verses on index cards and place them where

you will see them frequently. Read these passages aloud three times daily, committing them to memory. Ask God to reveal himself to you in your pain.

My Prayer for You

Father, during my most painful days, I depended on the prayers of others to carry my needs to your throne. It is my privilege and honor to come before your presence now on behalf of the one reading these words. In our pain, we come to you just as we are, weary and tired, just trying to make it from one moment to the next. When the pain is bad, we don't want to think of it never ending or of having to endure it much longer. When we look too far into the future, we become consumed with worry and dread, so help the one reading this to keep their eyes fixed firmly on you. Give this dear one strength to endure. We hold fast to our hope because you are faithful. In Jesus's name, amen.

Recommended Playlist

"Know You Will," Hillsong United, © 2021 by Hillsong Music and Resources, LLC

"Same God," Hannah Kerr, © 2021 by Black River Entertainment

"Control," Highlands Worship, © 2021 by Highlands Worship

"Miracle in Motion," Corey Voss, © 2020 by Integrity Music

4

Dark Night of the Soul

"When the pain gets this severe, I either want Jesus to heal me or take me home with him." I remember expressing this angst through tears to a friend on multiple occasions when I believed I neither could nor wanted to go on in such a state of despair. We prayed for days, weeks, months, and then years, and yet the pain continued to worsen and consume more of each day; some days it didn't even allow me time to be upright or out of bed. I openly and honestly explained to my husband that I wasn't suicidal and I didn't want to die; I just dreaded waking up in pain yet again and wanted to fall asleep and not wake up until the pain was gone. It didn't seem fair that God allowed me to endure such prolonged suffering to comfort others. Didn't he care as much about me as he did about them? In some ways, when I couldn't lift my head for the pain, I considered Jesus lucky—his earthly ministry lasted three years. He endured greater suffering than I ever would, but he knew his pain on this earth was time limited—I had no idea when or if my pain would end.

It wasn't just the physical pain that screamed its reminder all day long—it was the emotional pain from watching my children suffer their own trials; the relational pain from misunderstood motives and betrayal; the mental pain from beating myself up, believing I should have been a better wife, mother, friend, and child of God; and the spiritual pain that followed when God seemed silent in my darkest nights. People talk about "the dark night of the soul" as if it's a one-and-done event. It wasn't for me. My dark night was a plural! I suspect the same can be said about some of the heroes of the faith.

The Burden to Cover Up Our Pain

Sometimes pain and suffering are just that. They don't always make you stronger. They don't always build your character. Sometimes they just hurt. And there's space for that without trying to wrap it up in a pretty bow. Can we just acknowledge pain and heartache without trying to pretty them up to make ourselves and those around us feel better?

The pain always seems to be worse during the long, lonely night hours. People have seen me out and about or on social media and said, "I'm glad to see you're feeling better," when in fact the pain was raging, tears were stinging the backs of my eyes, and I was longing to crawl into bed but it wasn't an option. It makes me think of the 2019 Miss USA winner who smiled for the camera and was jovial during interviews just a day or two before she jumped from her Manhattan high-rise apartment to her death. It seems doubtful that her friends or family knew of the pain and despair she hid from others as her social media accounts portrayed fun, success, and beauty. But such is the truth for many who are in pain and who fear misunderstanding or dismissal if they vulnerably share about their painful existence.

Crawling in Faith

On the darkest, most painful nights, I've asked, "Lord, are you done with me?" I've wondered how David could have confidently declared, "Even though I walk through the darkest valley, I will fear no evil, for you are with me" (Ps. 23:4). David suffered in ways we can't imagine. Yet he ultimately declared the protection of God's shadow over his life: "Whoever dwells in the shelter of the Most High will rest in the shadow of the Almighty. I will say of the LORD, 'He is my refuge and my fortress, my God, in whom I trust'" (Ps. 91:1–2). What I most appreciate about David is his willingness to share the real and raw with God, understanding that God already knew his agonized thoughts anyway. He didn't succumb to the pressure to cover up his pain and only share his victories.

> Often, walking by faith comes from crawling in faith.

Often, walking by faith comes from crawling in faith. What's important is that we hold on to our faith. Toddlers first learn to crawl and then stumble along on uncertain feet, often falling along the way, and yet parents don't scold them for their inability to run with wild abandon. Neither does our heavenly Father scold us as we crawl in our faith before we gain our spiritual balance. Instead, the cry of his heart is "Come to me, all you who are weary and burdened, and I will give you rest. Take my yoke upon you and learn from me, for I am gentle and humble in heart, and you will find rest for your souls" (Matt. 11:28–29). God doesn't put unrealistic expectations on us—we do.

Hope during the Dark Night

Have you ever had one of those days, weeks, months, or even years when your painful experience seemed to climb from nagging to excruciating or worse? When things felt hopeless? What do you do then? How do you find hope when pain is unremitting and life seems dark?

The statistics are staggering. Over twenty-three million Americans suffer from anxiety disorders, almost eighteen million Americans suffer from clinical depression, and rates of suicide have skyrocketed exponentially over the last couple of years, especially among teens and young adults. Every day countless people endure feelings of fear and hopelessness. Patients agonize over diagnoses, treatments, and prognoses. Parents worry about keeping their jobs, putting food on the table, having a roof over their family's heads, and providing a good education for their children. Life crises often trigger or escalate pain, and pain is seldom without at least an undercurrent of worry or anxiety about a pain-filled future.

Sadly, accolades, awards, and even wealth don't prevent pain or hopelessness, as the life of our friend Job reveals. Often, in fact, the more successful we are, the emptier we feel and the more pressure we entertain to *do* more, *be* more, and *have* more, all while pain compromises our ability to do, be, and have. Whitney Houston, Heath Ledger, Prince, Michael Jackson—these celebrities and many more succumbed intentionally or unintentionally to drug overdoses while attempting to soothe some type of pain.

My pain has spun out of control plenty of times. Those times don't mesh well with my in-charge, get-it-done, push-through personality. Sometimes my initial response isn't the most appropriate. I've often gotten tied up in frustration—or agitation or anxiety—which has then led me to feel overwhelmed or angry. When pain has stretched out over time, I've despaired, feeling hopeless and wishing Jesus would just take me to heaven. Those dark nights of the soul bring me to the vulnerable questions, *Where is God when it hurts? Doesn't God care? Why doesn't*

God heal? Will I be okay? Will this actually work out for good?
Will the hurting ever stop?

When things seem devastating, we get to choose how we will respond. We can employ the same strategies modeled for us in God's Word. For example, God richly rewarded Abraham for his obedience, and Abraham is now known as the father of faith.

The dark night of the soul stems from the despair and hopelessness we experience when viewing our circumstances from our own limited and isolated perspective, yammering for an immediate resolution. We become frustrated, discouraged, and hopeless when we lack the insight or peace that comes from viewing things through our heavenly Father's eternal perspective. I'm comforted to know that God knew we would struggle, so he gave us his Word to instruct us and guide us, and he gave us godly women and men to lead by example. Otherwise I would be even more tempted than I already am to fall into a pit of shame when my hope lags. Many of the biblical greats, including Hannah and Abraham, experienced similar situations and emotions and offer lessons to us on our pain journey regarding positive coping mechanisms amid painful trials.

Hannah's Example

Hannah's story exemplifies hopelessness, despair, and grief. First Samuel 1 tells us that Hannah was barren following her marriage, which caused her great pain on several levels. In her culture, Hannah's personal, social, and marital value was pegged to her fertility. In addition, her polygamous husband had another wife who bore him children and who used that status to continually diminish Hannah. Year after year, Hannah returned to the temple during the family's regular pilgrimages to make appropriate sacrifices and implore God for an answer to her prayer and for relief from her suffering. Hannah longed for things to change in her pain journey. "In her deep anguish Hannah prayed to the LORD, weeping bitterly" (v. 10). Hannah didn't hide her despair, hopelessness, or pain but instead took them to the Lord.

When Eli, the priest, questioned her at the temple, thinking that in her quiet mumblings she was drunk, Hannah relayed her grief: "I am a woman who is deeply troubled. I have not been drinking wine or beer; I was pouring out my soul to the LORD. Do not take your servant for a wicked woman; I have been praying here out of my great anguish and grief" (vv. 15–16). After Hannah poured out her heart to God, "she went her way and ate something, and her face was no longer downcast" (v. 18). Ultimately, God blessed Hannah with a child, Samuel, who was a great prophet of the nation of Israel. Without knowing of God's eventual blessing, though, Hannah's time with God had a threefold effect on her: It allowed her to "go her way," or resume her ordinary life; her appetite returned; and her affect was lifted. In the act of bringing her pain before God, Hannah found a level of relief. Hannah's prayers were associated with her presence in the temple. We don't have that restriction and can approach our heavenly Father at any time in any place.

The writer of Hebrews tells us, "Let us then approach God's throne of grace with confidence, so that we may receive mercy and find grace to help us in our time of need" (4:16).

We can take an important lesson from Hannah. In our pain, we must not allow ourselves to become bitter or isolated but continue to pray for God's healing and worship him while we wait.

Abraham's Example

Abraham experienced hopelessness and despair but acts as a role model for those of us enduring the dark night of the soul now. "When everything was hopeless, Abraham believed anyway, deciding to live not on the basis of what he saw he *couldn't* do but on what God said he *would* do" (Rom. 4:18 MSG, italics in the original). Abraham's example acts as a guide to us today and offers us three powerful lessons:

1. **When Abraham felt hopeless, he believed anyway,** despite what he saw and felt in his human experience.

   Hebrews 11:1 says, "Now faith is confidence in what we hope for and assurance about what we do not see." Abraham maintained his faith and kept believing in the sovereignty of God, the goodness of God, the provision of God, and the faithfulness of God, even when he didn't see an answer to his pain.

   Our culture, our flesh, and our spiritual enemy constantly sow doubt in our minds about these truths of God that Abraham believed. When we cannot see God's hand at work, it's then that we must trust his character and remember that he has never gone back on a promise before, so he will be faithful.

   Perhaps our key to trusting God is best found in Psalm 56:3–4: "When I am afraid, I put my trust in you. In God, whose word I praise—in God I trust and am not afraid. What can mere mortals do to me?"

2. **When everything around him appeared hopeless, Abraham was intentional.** Even when Abraham felt hopeless, he believed anyway and fell back on his previously established and practiced expressions of faith. Abraham crafted his life to reflect his beliefs. He was intentional. As far as we can tell, when God told Abraham to leave his land, Abraham settled in a new place when he was seventy-five years old without questioning God's directive. As Abraham traveled through this faraway and strange place, he built several altars as reminders to

himself of God's promise and presence, and at times he returned to those altars.

When crises come, they are easier to manage when we've intentionally decided ahead of time what we believe and how we will respond and then practice these decisions. We can't trust our emotions when we're in crisis or feeling angry, anxious, down, despairing, or helpless, so deciding ahead of time how we will respond will buoy our strength when the hurricanes of pain threaten to take us under.

Taking the time to know God's Word before pain or crises hit cements the hope we have in God. But it requires intentionality. We will all face difficult times at some point, but what makes them hard is that we rarely get any forewarning. Psalm 119:50 describes the value of deeply knowing the Word of God when we are suffering: "My comfort in my suffering is this: Your promise preserves my life."

3. **When life seemed hopeless, Abraham focused his attention on God rather than on his problems.** Abraham decided to live his life based on what *God* could do rather than what Abraham could do in his own strength. Sarah was barren, and Abraham despaired over not having children to inherit his estate. God prompted Abraham to look up and count the stars then promised he would give Abraham that many offspring as part of his spiritual lineage. Scripture records, "Abram believed the LORD, and he credited it to him as righteousness" (Gen. 15:6).

Later, God called Abraham to do the unthinkable: to lay his son, Isaac, for whom Abraham and Sarah had waited many years, on the altar as a sacrifice to God. Abraham didn't question, complain to, or argue with

God but rather, in faith, did as God commanded. Even as Abraham and Isaac journeyed up the mountain and Isaac questioned his father about what they would offer as a sacrifice, Abraham answered in faith: "God himself will provide the lamb for the burnt offering, my son" (22:8). He believed God was greater than his circumstance. God did not disappoint. He rewarded Abraham's faithfulness throughout his life and made him a father of nations.

In the middle of our pain and anxiety, we can't see our whole scenario from beginning to resolution. But God can. Rather than focusing on your problems, focus on the Problem Solver. Focusing on God brings great rewards. Romans 15:13 reminds us of such rewards: "May the God of hope fill you with all joy and peace as you trust in him, so that you may overflow with hope by the power of the Holy Spirit." It's God who fills us with hope, joy, and peace *when* we trust in him. We will return to this concept of focusing on God in the next chapter and talk a little more about how to do that.

Using Abraham as our example, let's believe God, be intentional in our thoughts and words, and focus our attention on God rather than on our circumstances. Let's meditate day and night on God's promises and his Word, particularly with respect to healing. Whether our pain is physical, emotional, spiritual, relational, grief, or secondary, we need God to heal and bind up our wounds, the source of our pain. Here are three Scriptures that can build trust and give you hope when your pain needs healing or your attention needs focusing:

> He gives strength to the weary
> and increases the power of the weak. (Isa. 40:29)

> But he was pierced for our transgressions,
>   he was crushed for our iniquities;
> the punishment that brought us peace was on him,
>   and by his wounds we are healed. (Isa. 53:5)

> Nevertheless, I will bring health and healing to it; I will heal my people and will let them enjoy abundant peace and security. (Jer. 33:6)

Remember God's Faithfulness

During the dark nights of my soul, I really didn't want to go on if it meant waking up each day in the same condition as when I'd laid my head down the night before. The nights were long and most certainly lonely and despairing as the enemy's taunts filled my room: *This is the best it'll ever be. Tomorrow will be worse than today because you're not sleeping. You're no longer thriving . . . in fact, you're barely surviving. Just give up—it would be better for everyone.* Like Hannah, I had to make the conscious choice to continue calling out to God, asking for his voice to be the loudest one I heard. I reminded myself and God of the many promises he's made, and I reminded myself of his faithfulness. I also had to consciously refute the doubts I heard echoing in my mind from my own warped perspective, from our culture's misdirected priorities and ideals, and from the active spiritual enemy we all deal with.

I've had to realize that feelings aren't facts and that while facts are compelling, they aren't the same as truth. Just because I feel like God is far away or like he doesn't love me during my painful trials, that doesn't mean God is distant or that I am unloved. That's when we have to search for truth.

Cling to the Promises of God

Second Corinthians 1:20 tells us, "For no matter how many promises God has made, they are 'Yes' in Christ. And so through him the 'Amen' is spoken by us to the glory of God." While it is difficult to trust other people or earthly institutions, we can trust God to be faithful in keeping his promises. But here's the interesting thing: We get to partner with God in seeing his promises fulfilled. We see the guarantee of God's fulfillment of his promises in Jesus, but when we add our "amen," which means "yes" or "so be it," to his promises, it brings God glory because we are exercising our faith while we wait for his promises to be fulfilled. This is consistent with the Hebrew word *towdah*, which means giving God thanks and praise *in advance*, when we have yet to see what he's going to do. This is what Abraham did. "Abram believed the LORD, and he credited it to him as righteousness" (Gen. 15:6). When we add our "amen" to the promises of God and endorse God's promises to be fulfilled in our lives, we must release the how and the when to God's sovereign plan. All we can do is say "so be it," then wait on it to happen in his perfect way and in his perfect time.

> When we add our "amen" to his promises, it brings God glory because we are exercising our faith while we wait for his promises to be fulfilled.

If we're experiencing no change in our present circumstances or seeing little hope for change in the future, we can remind ourselves of God's faithfulness in the past. God has always been faithful in the past; we have no reason to doubt his faithfulness in our future, and that's where we put our trust. As you believe in God, intentionally pursue a relationship with him, find him in his Word, choose to focus on the Problem Solver rather than the problem, and add your "amen" to his promises, may you experience his hope that prevails and find satisfaction in the God who is sovereign, good, abundant, and faithful.

The Hem of His Garment

> But each day the LORD pours his unfailing love upon me,
> and through each night I sing his songs,
> praying to God who gives me life.
>
> Psalm 42:8 NLT

Your Rx

1. God's goodness, faithfulness, and abundant provision are attributes that don't necessarily show up when and where we want to see them in specific areas of our lives. We *can*, however, look for them elsewhere in our lives and in the lives of those around us and then pray that God will help us better recognize his presence. Where do you see these gifts of God in your life and in the lives of others? Thank God for them and ask him to help you more easily identify his goodness, faithfulness, provision, and presence in your life.

2. Consider the examples of Hannah and Abraham. How can you apply the lessons from their stories to your pain journey?

3. Look up Psalms 91:1–2; 119:50; and Romans 15:13. Write these verses on index cards and place them where you will see them frequently. Read these passages aloud

three times daily, committing them to memory. Ask God to reveal himself to you in your pain.

My Prayer for You

Father, my heart is burdened for your dear child reading these words who may be enduring their own dark-night-of-the-soul, painful experience. You know every skinned knee and bruised heart your children endure. Forgive us for those times when we struggle to give thanks in all things, including our pain. Comfort your child in the lonely, painful nights when the whispers of the enemy are deafening, and worry, fear, anxiety, doubt, and dread come knocking on their heart's door. Hold them close in your protective arms and let them hear your heartbeat of love for them. Blanket them in your peace and bring them joy in the morning while we wait for you to fulfill your promises. In Jesus's name, amen.

Recommended Playlist

"Every Line," NewSpring Worship, © 2017 by Dream Worship

"Promises," Shane & Shane, © 2020 by The Worship Initiative

"Questions," 7eventh Time Down, © 2020 by BEC Recordings

"Need You Now," Plumb, © 2012 by Curb Records, Inc.

5

Choose Your Focus

I considered my current condition. How did I get here? *My physical pain increased from occasional to daily and then from occurring mostly in the late afternoon or evening to occurring all day and interfering with sleep. Betrayal, lies, and rejection in relationships compounded the pain. Emotionally, I felt weighed down, like a boat by its anchor, with no strength left to pull it aboard. Spiritually, God seemed uncharacteristically distant and quiet, despite my pleas for him to speak to me.*

"Normal" seemed like a distant memory, with grief and loss replacing it. I held out little hope that normal would ever return. I felt tempted to give in to hopelessness, except I knew that was what the enemy desired and that nothing is ever truly hopeless when we trust the God of the universe to always have our best interests at heart.

Would normal ever return? Could normal ever return after the hurtful words lingering in the memory of my heart? After structural changes had occurred in my body? After people I loved died? Normal as I knew it would never return, but what would my new normal hold?

The Focus of the Wilderness Experience

A friend and I talked recently about the "wilderness" times of our lives. One definition of *wilderness* is "an uncultivated, uninhabited, or inhospitable region."[1] Have you ever been there? Perhaps you're there now. What did you learn while you were there? What would you tell someone who currently walks there?

I equate periods of intense, prolonged pain and suffering to wilderness experiences in part because the pain sufferer often feels alone, helpless, and despairing in their plight. We experience secondary pain inflicted by others when we interpret their messages as their saying, "Quit complaining"; "We're tired of hearing about it—do something about it instead"; or even, "You brought this on yourself." When we interpret others' messages that way, we tend to withdraw and isolate to self-protect, which only exacerbates our feelings of loneliness.

We wander around pain's wilderness not wanting to cultivate the land because we don't want to stay there. And that region feels inhospitable—nothing about it begs us to find a comfortable seat with our favorite beverage and just sit in awe and wonder of the land and the adventures to be experienced there. We want to run as fast and as far away from there as possible and never turn back for another experience or to make a new memory.

Our painful wilderness periods can also be considered refining fires. Such times aren't pleasant, yet they produce lasting fruit in our lives. Hebrews 12:11 assures us, "No discipline seems pleasant at the time, but painful. Later on, however, it produces a harvest of righteousness and peace for those who have been trained by it." Pain sufferers often believe the misconception that they must have done something wrong to displease God and that their suffering is a form of his punishment. Yet that's inconsistent with truth. Discipline does not equate to punishment. It functions as training to better equip us for battle. In God's great love for us, he trains us, so we learn to experience his best for us, ultimately and eternally.

Wilderness journeys are uncomfortable at best and excruciatingly painful and lonely at worst, but they are wanderings that produce stretching and incomparable growth. It's in the wilderness where God most has our attention to teach us to depend on him rather than ourselves or others. People may disappoint, frustrate, reject, or abandon us, but God hunkers down and remains in the wilderness with us. As we lean into him, he walks the wilderness journey alongside us. We won't always *feel* his presence, but we can *know* and trust

> Discipline does not equate to punishment. It functions as training to better equip us for battle.

that he is there. When we come out of the wilderness, we can look in the rearview mirror and see how our relationship with God grew stronger.

Because of the isolation of the wilderness, God can more easily get our attention there than he can when he's competing with other people or distractions. It is in the wilderness where he teaches us that everything we need is in him and that he is faithful even when we don't understand his answers. It's a very intimate place where we can learn to know him for who he really is. The wilderness is often called "a dry and thirsty land" (Ps. 63:1 KJV), and in that place, we become thirsty for a more intimate relationship with the Lord.

Consider the Israelites and their time in the wilderness. They assumed upon leaving Egypt that they would soon be in the promised land. Their extended wilderness journey resulted in a loss of normal and a sense of grief. Their complaints focused on their desire to return to normal (see Num. 13–14). Isn't that true in each of our pain journeys—our complaints result from the desire to return to normal, the normal that existed prior to our painful wilderness journey?

Paul understood this as well. As one who endured much loss, he recognized that his old normal was being replaced by a new normal, which included a life more energized and enlivened by God's growing presence in it. In Philippians 3, Paul enumerates being a "Hebrew of the Hebrews" (v. 5) as one of his qualifications for earthly status and pride. He sounds like he's boasting, but two verses later Paul states, "Whatever were gains to me I now consider loss for the sake of Christ" (v. 7). Then he adds, "I consider everything a loss because of the surpassing worth of knowing Christ Jesus my Lord, for whose sake I have lost all things. I consider them garbage, that I may gain Christ" (v. 8). He concludes this passage by saying, "Forgetting what is behind and straining toward what is ahead, I press on toward the goal to win the prize for which God has called me heavenward in Christ Jesus" (vv. 13–14).

The Focus of Eternity

God never shies away from the hard stuff. He forewarned us about the trials and difficulties this life would bring, and he's given us clues to aid in our understanding and appreciation of his ways from an eternal perspective. In 2 Corinthians 4, pain sufferers are given encouragement straight from God's heart: "For our present troubles are small and won't last very long. Yet they produce for us a glory that vastly outweighs them and will last forever! So we don't look at the troubles we can see now; rather, we fix our gaze on things that cannot be seen. For the things we see now will soon be gone, but the things we cannot see will last forever" (vv. 17–18 NLT).

When we discuss pain and suffering and consider God's truth, *small* is a relative term. A time-limited term. A term equated with growth. Our pain may seem unbearable, yet we read of the apostle Paul's "small" troubles, which included being beaten nearly to death on multiple occasions, enduring shipwrecks, being imprisoned, and eventually becoming a martyr. He had a close relationship with the Lord, but we don't know if he knew the fate that awaited him when he wrote those words to the Corinthians. Yet his point was that all our suffering becomes "small" when contrasted with eternal glory.

In the depths of my pain, I've never found comfort in the cliché "This too shall pass" because there are relatively few guarantees that pain will pass in this lifetime or that healing will come this side of heaven or that we will want the new normal when "this" passes. I'm not sure grief ever passes, although the intensity may lessen over time. Yet the truth of that statement is that the sun will come out again, and God has never failed on his promises to us yet. Paul's words encourage us that our troubles, as painful as they are, will not last forever, that our eternity will be pain-free, and that we have that relief to look forward to. Yet, while we endure the pain journey, we can shift our focus by asking God, "What do you want to teach me in this painful wilderness?" knowing that he never wastes our pain.

Normal Isn't Returning—Focus on a New Normal

Throughout the global pandemic, I repeatedly heard people question, "When will we get back to normal?" The truth is, we won't. We are forced to adapt to a new normal. There are some who will wear masks forever. And we will likely never think about a virus the same again. Many will never return to work, and some will only return remotely. We can't unlearn the things we learned during that time.

Pain brings us to the same desire and conclusion. We desire to return to our prepain state, but that often isn't possible. Whether we're talking about physical, emotional, relational, or one of the other types of pain, we can't return to the old normal. We've learned lessons along the journey. We conclude who the safe people are in our life. We're forced to go on after a loved one dies. Frequently, we can't undo the physical damage in our body. Health care too often treats our symptoms without addressing the root of our pain. What we can do rather than bemoaning the losses or changes in our life is choose our focus—on the new normal—and in doing so, establish some more positive coping mechanisms to carry us through our pain journey.

Mindset—What We Focus on Grows

When I discovered I was expecting our first child, I knew no one else who was pregnant. We waited quite a while to start our family, so most of my friends were through the pregnancy stage by then. But it seemed that everywhere I looked, I noticed pregnant women, probably because I was so focused on my own pregnancy. Similarly, when my husband and I were looking for a new car, each day we noticed many people driving the same models we were considering. The incidence was probably no different, yet we were more attuned to those models because our search focused on them.

I've realized that whatever we focus on grows. When I focus on my pain, before long all I can see is the bad. That leads to feelings of hopelessness. But the more I focus on the goodness of God, the more I experience his good heart toward me, which offers hope. When all we can see is our pain, we lose sight of God. One of the greatest challenges I've encountered in treating patients has been teaching them the importance of our mindset and what we spend time focusing on. When we feel anxious or discouraged, focusing on those emotions depresses our feelings and our mood. Choosing to smile, even during painful difficulties, doesn't mean we don't hurt. And it doesn't mean we're being fake or insincere. It means we're choosing to focus on everything we can be grateful for—our blessings, the simple joys sprinkled around us by our heavenly Father—rather than focusing on the painful trials.

> **When all we can see is our pain, we lose sight of God.**

The apostle Paul shares the importance of focusing on God's truth: "Until I get there, focus on reading the Scriptures to the church, encouraging the believers, and teaching them" (1 Tim. 4:13 NLT). When we focus on the truth, our entire day seems so much better, brighter, and more encouraging. *What we focus on grows.* That doesn't mean we won't experience difficult moments within a given day but that we'll be less prone to let those moments ruin an entire day. In negative events, God is still present, and he still provides.

The Neuropsychology behind What We Focus On

Our thought patterns impact our brain. Consider the idea that our thoughts carve mental pathways that our future thoughts travel on. The more we entertain certain thoughts—whether they're positive, such as "God loves me," or negative, such as "I'm so stupid"—the more we believe them and the more entrenched those pathways become in our brain. I often tell patients, "Pay attention to your thoughts because *you* are listening!"

Only when we stop and consider our thoughts can we tell whether they are consistent with what God says. When our thoughts are not consistent with God's thoughts, we tend to be more negative not only toward ourselves but also toward others.

The thoughts we think impact our physical, mental, and spiritual health. "A tranquil heart gives life to the flesh, but envy makes the bones rot" (Prov. 14:30 ESV). To see positive changes in your health, relationships, finances, mood, and relationship with God, take control of your thoughts. The battle for our thoughts is one of the largest battles we face. When we line up our thoughts with the thoughts and promises of God, it gives our spirit the opportunity to renew our thoughts and our attitudes.

Focus on the Problem Solver Rather Than the Problems

Jesus warns us that we will all suffer trouble in this world, but he wants us to understand and appreciate that our focus should not be on the trouble but on his peace and the victory that we have in him. "I have told you these things, so that in me you may have peace. In this world you will have trouble. But take heart! I have overcome the world" (John 16:33). Focusing on God rather than our problems comes down to intentionally choosing to recognize God's presence, provision, and promises alongside the facts of our situation. Let me provide an example: When I received the call from my doctor that my biopsy had come back positive for cancer, the enemy tempted me to worry and become fearful and anxious by directing my thoughts to all the what-if questions: *What if we didn't catch it in time? What if treatment isn't effective? What if the prognosis is worse than the doctor suspects?* Each of those questions caused me to focus on the circumstance of being given a cancer diagnosis.

I had to broaden my perspective and consider other pertinent truths: *This did not take God by surprise, and he already knows how he's going to get me through this. God is still on his throne and is still in the miracle-making and healing business today. God promises to be my Healer, and he promises to supply my every need.* By de-emphasizing the circumstances and emphasizing (and choosing to believe) what God has promised in his Word, I was able to have peace through the process and leave my unknown future in the hands of my known God.

How Do We Truly Give Our Problems to God?

We often forget to focus on the enormity of our God living among us and inside us and all that he has already accomplished for us. That's where some form of remembrance can be incredibly helpful, even if it is only journaled words scratched on a notepad to remind us of all he has already done and to help us trust what he remains capable of doing. Giving our problems to God is a matter of choice and intentionality. Much like the man in Mark 9:24 telling Jesus that he believed but then asking him to help his unbelief, giving our problems to God starts with a willing heart.

When our heart is willing to give God our problems, I believe that God, by the power of the Holy Spirit, has an open door to remind us of the truth we know. When he reminds us of the truth of his Word and of the many promises he's given us, we declare our willingness to trust what God says more than what our circumstances suggest.

When we slip—and we all do—we repent and confess our lapse into worry, fear, anxiety, doubt, or discouragement and ask God to strengthen our resolve to leave our problems with him and not pick them up again. He is patient and willing to forgive.

Staying Focused on God and the Things of God

The apostle Paul tells us what we should focus on in Philippians 4:8–9: "Finally, brothers and sisters, whatever is true, whatever is noble, whatever is right, whatever is pure, whatever is lovely, whatever is admirable—if anything is excellent or praiseworthy—think about such things. Whatever you have learned or received or heard from me, or seen in me—put it into practice. And the God of peace will be with you."

Because God is always good and is only capable of good, when we focus on what he deems to be good things, we won't be able to keep ourselves from focusing on him, all that he is, and all that he has done. When our focus is on God, our thoughts, feelings, attitudes, beliefs, and behaviors will all follow, and it will be difficult to have a bad day.

How Do I Stay Focused on God?

Staying focused on God in today's overly busy, ever-changing world is not easy. Distractions, demands, and even our emotions can pull us away from a regular investment in knowing God more deeply. Below are several ways you can draw closer to God. Don't feel like you need to tackle each one immediately or like you must find a quick change in your relationship with him. Start small and invest time and energy intentionally and daily.

1. **Desire a deeper relationship with God.** I have found that when life is going well, we can unconsciously slip into a mindset in which we believe or behave as though we can handle things on our own rather than depending on God. It takes greater diligence and intentionality to seek God when things are going well than when they are

not, but establishing that rhythm of relationship helps to provide a sense of God's presence and participation when things are not going well. When you know how to look and listen, seeing and hearing God in the middle of the storm is so much easier!

> Then you will call upon me and come and pray to me, and I will hear you. You will seek me and find me, when you seek me with all your heart. I will be found by you, declares the LORD. (Jer. 29:12–14 ESV)

2. **Receive and walk in God's forgiveness.** The enemy wants us to wallow in guilt, shame, and condemnation. But once we've repented and confessed our sin and our failures to God, we can know that he has forgiven us. God's forgiveness is like a birthday or Christmas present offered by a parent to their child—it must be received to be of any good. Getting over ourselves and recognizing that Jesus paid the price and that forgiveness is truly and completely available is an earthshaking experience that is hard to understand or accept without the leading of God's Holy Spirit. But in seeking his forgiveness, receiving it, understanding it, and accepting it, we see how unbelievably gracious God is.

> O Lord, you are so good, so ready to forgive, so full of unfailing love for all who ask for your help. (Ps. 86:5 NLT)

3. **Guard your eyes, ears, and heart.** God tells us that we will be exposed to many things in this world, and we must take care what we allow in our eyes, ears, mind,

and heart, whether it be from TV, radio, books, magazines, social media, music, or even conversations with others.

> My son, pay attention to what I say;
>> turn your ear to my words.
> Do not let them out of your sight,
>> keep them within your heart;
> for they are life to those who find them
>> and health to one's whole body.
> Above all else, guard your heart,
>> for everything you do flows from it.
> Keep your mouth free of perversity;
>> keep corrupt talk far from your lips.
> Let your eyes look straight ahead;
>> fix your gaze directly before you.
> Give careful thought to the paths for your feet
>> and be steadfast in all your ways.
> Do not turn to the right or the left;
>> keep your foot from evil. (Prov. 4:20–27)

4. **Seek to walk by the Holy Spirit.** Being filled with the Spirit produces good fruit and helps keep our focus on the things that God deems most important. When we focus on God and are led by his Spirit, we will be filled with the Holy Spirit and exemplify the fruit of the Spirit for others to see.

> But the Holy Spirit produces this kind of fruit in our lives: love, joy, peace, patience, kindness, goodness, faithfulness, gentleness, and self-control. There is no law against these things! (Gal. 5:22–23 NLT)

5. **Stay attached to the vine (Jesus) through regular Bible study and prayer.** Jesus explained how we can maintain our focus on God rather than on our problems when he shared how important it is for us to abide in him. That includes thinking about him, what he preached, what he promised, and what he did, with an emphasis on trying to become more like him. Consider recording for your future reference and encouragement the insights God gives you and the times you see his hand at work.

> I have loved you even as the Father has loved me. Remain in my love. When you obey my commandments, you remain in my love, just as I obey my Father's commandments and remain in his love. I have told you these things so that you will be filled with my joy. Yes, your joy will overflow! (John 15:9–11 NLT)

6. **Study and focus on the promises and truth of God.** In my most recent book, *Today Is Going to Be a Good Day*, I emphasized the importance of focusing on the truth of God's Word, especially the many promises he gives us. Even painful days can be good days when we focus on God and his promises. We have been given the gift of the Holy Spirit to remind us of all truth, but he cannot remind us of that which we don't know, so it's up to us to study God's Word and learn what it says.

> And you will know the truth, and the truth will set you free. (John 8:32 NLT)

> Lead me by your truth and teach me,
>   for you are the God who saves me.
> All day long I put my hope in you. (Ps. 25:5 NLT)

7. **Worship and praise open your heart to receive from the Lord.** When I was going through a major health crisis and in the pit of depression, I found it hard to even desire to praise and worship God, despite knowing its importance. Scripture reminds us that God inhabits the praises of his people (see Ps. 22:3 KJV). As we praise and worship, our hearts become more receptive to the work of the Holy Spirit.

> Honor the LORD for the glory of his name.
>   Worship the LORD in the splendor of his holiness.
>   (Ps. 29:2 NLT)

> Why am I discouraged?
>   Why is my heart so sad?
> I will put my hope in God!
>   I will praise him again—
>   my Savior and my God! (Ps. 42:11 NLT)

Are you hurting? Suffering with pain? When pain is loud, threatening, and convincing, we must trust God's presence and provision, not our pain. Our pain lies to us, but God never will. He is with us, he is for us, and he will bring us through. Trust that.

The Hem of His Garment

"The glory of this present house will be greater than the glory of the former house," says the LORD Almighty. "And in this place I will grant peace," declares the LORD Almighty.

Haggai 2:9

Your Rx
---

1. Pray and ask God to reveal the truth about where your focus has been. Then prayerfully ask him to redirect your focus to his character, his promises, and his truth as they relate to your pain.

2. Consider the different ways mentioned in the chapter to stay focused on God. Commit to implementing one or two of them at this stage in your pain journey.

3. Look up 2 Corinthians 4:17–18; Philippians 4:8–9; and John 15:9–11. Write the verses on index cards and place them where you will see them frequently. Read these passages aloud three times daily, committing them to memory. Ask God to reveal himself to you in your pain.

My Prayer for You

Father, my heart is heavy for the one holding this book in their hands right now. I'm grateful your heart is inclined toward this precious child of yours as well. In the painful wilderness experiences, when all seems lost and unlikely to return to normal, help them to focus on the only constant in their lives: you. Jesus warned us that we would face trials in this world but encouraged us to take heart because he has already won the victory for us. Help your precious child to keep their eyes on the eternal prize. If life will never return to normal as they know it, help them to recognize a new normal, one with your greater presence. Open their eyes of faith. In Jesus's name, amen.

Recommended Playlist

"I Believe in You," JJ Heller, © 2021 by Stone Table
   Records

"Be My Shalom," Evan Craft, © 2020 by Evan Craft
   Music

"New Normal," Cade Thompson, © 2021 by Red Street
   Records

"Honest," Kyndal Inskeep, © 2022 by Song House

6

Relating to God in Pain

I paced the surgical waiting room, my mind and body on hyperalert. Whenever someone stood to get a cup of coffee, my gaze reflexively followed them. Whenever someone signed in or out at the waiting-room desk, my head jerked to attention. Whenever a name was called over the speaker, my mind did a double take to ensure it wasn't mine. And every time a surgeon walked through the doors to confer with a family member, I rose, even though I knew it would still be hours before I would hear anything.

The surgeon finally walked through the doors, yanked the cap off his head, and met my gaze. I searched his eyes, preparing myself for the worst. Approximately ten years into our marriage, my husband was undergoing surgery for a very rare form of abdominal cancer. Having been warned that only one in four patients survives the surgery, we had approached the procedure with caution. Now I wondered whether he was the one or among the three. "The surgery was about as successful as possible. You may see him for a few minutes."

Suddenly I thought of nothing and everything simultaneously. He survived—at least for the time being. Thank you, God. But now what? I needed to see him for it to be real. I had waited the better part of twenty-four hours from the time they rolled him away from me down the hall to surgery until he was settled into the ICU where I would be able to see him, to touch him, to talk to him. Waiting in the surgical waiting room, I'd lost all sense of time. I was too nervous to eat, and I couldn't sleep, afraid I would miss the surgeon and his report. The stream of sunlight piercing through the pinhole in the window blinds surprised me. Daylight. It was daylight. He had survived another day. The last time I had seen him, we'd held hands, prayed, and praised God for his medical team. And then I watched them wheel him to surgery while I stood alone holding his belongings.

The various beeps and whirs of ICU machines monitoring his vital signs jerked me back to the present. But nothing could have prepared me for what I saw next. My eyes were drawn to the floor. I gasped as I saw a large pool of his blood expanding against the stark-white tile floor. In shock, I looked up to see my husband's body, nearly unrecognizable. He seemed dwarfed compared to the bed. Pale. Covered in wires and tubes.

"Oh God, no. Please no. He doesn't deserve this. He's been through so much. Don't make him go through any more . . ." I sobbed as I fell to my knees beside his bed. A nurse escorted me to an ICU waiting-room chair where I lived for the next ten days, save for ten minutes every six hours when I was permitted to see him, hold his hand, pray with him. My tears and my prayers continued. "God, he didn't do anything to deserve this. He's been through so much already. Please don't let him die. And please don't let him hurt anymore. Please let me take this pain and torture for him . . ."

As I prayed, I sensed God whisper to my heart, That's what my Son did. He took the pain and torture that would have been yours and went through it on the cross for you. He shed his blood for you, so you didn't have to. It's what love does. *In that moment, I pictured the blood I'd seen on the floor as Jesus's blood at the foot of the cross. It was his sacrifice. He didn't deserve to be tortured or to die. He did it willingly, as a gift. It's what love does. Had we not gone through that painful trial, I likely never would've related to Christ's shed blood in such a personal way. Jesus knows and understands my pain, our pain, all of it.*

Our Setbacks Are God's Setup

Our pain produces vulnerability, and our vulnerability makes us easy prey for the assaults of those negative forces that are always present: our own fleshly desire for comfort and control, the popular cultural lure of personal satisfaction and comfort, and the active spiritual enemy who opposes us. These assaults, magnified through the vulnerability that pain creates, produce fear and frustration, which many of us display as anger. We often project this anger onto God, blaming him for either not preventing our pain or not fixing it.

A friend and I recently joked via text that we've both occasionally wanted to fire the Holy Spirit. If the Holy Spirit is considered the Great Comforter, why doesn't he comfort us in the depths of our despair? Maybe you've wondered that also. If so, you're not alone. Moses and his fellow wilderness wanderers did too:

> They said to Moses, "Why did you bring us out here to die in the wilderness? Weren't there enough graves for us in Egypt? What have you done to us? Why did you make us leave Egypt?" (Exod. 14:11 NLT)

The newly liberated Hebrew people wanted to fire Moses, or worse. But look at the basis for their questions and accusations. They blamed Moses as if he had forced them to leave Egypt. And they exaggerated their discomfort in claiming that he brought them into the wilderness to die. Amid painful trials, we search for answers, we long for explanations, and we want to understand the why and how, not only to make sense of our suffering but perhaps also to prevent it from reoccurring.

We realized for years after my husband's diagnosis and treatment that we literally held our breath prior to subsequent medical appointments, tests, and treatments because we never wanted to be taken off guard or have our world rocked like that again. That's when it's crucial to look past the pain of our circumstance and our own warped perspective to see the presence of God and the offer of his perspective in our pain. Our pain becomes a setup for us to see God's truth, character, and provision in a fresh way.

Perspectives from Pain

Feeling Abandoned by God

Our enemies—our own fallen way of thinking, the influence of the world around us, and our active spiritual enemy—love to suggest God has abandoned us, for then we will reject God and stop resisting their way of thinking. When we don't receive answers to life's painful questions, we tend to retreat, hide, harden our hearts, or confabulate to come up with answers to our unanswered questions. God's ways are not our ways, and he determines if, when, and how our questions receive answers. But it's crucial to remember that his silence doesn't equate to abandonment, regardless of what is whispered in our metaphorical ears.

The Hebrews of Exodus felt abandoned by God despite his miraculous presence through the pillar of cloud by day and the pillar of fire by night (see Exod. 13:21–22). In reading this story now, we are amazed that they either couldn't see or seriously discounted *God's physical presence*. How could they miss this? They saw the Red Sea part. God provided them with a supernatural, 24/7 billboard of the pillar of fire by night and the cloud by day to guide them. They ate manna from heaven daily for decades. Their shoes didn't wear out. How could they have missed God's presence and provision? But they did. They grumbled among *themselves*. They looked to each other and their recent past in Egypt for their standard of comfort and for what life should look like. Their specific questions remained unanswered in the way they desired, yet God was not only present but provided light, protection, sustenance, and other necessities despite their desire for more familiar conditions. I don't want to make light of the discomfort of the Hebrews of Exodus. What they experienced was certainly traumatic and difficult. The questions in their minds were valid, but the assumptions they made and their attitudes in expressing their fears and doubts betrayed their perspective.

The questions we ask in the dark closet of pain attest to our need for God and our desire for relationship with him: *I know he can heal, so why doesn't he? The Bible says God is love, but does he love me? And if he loves me, why does he leave me to suffer alone?*

David had a similar plea: "My God, my God, why have you forsaken me? Why are you so far from saving me, so far from my cries of anguish?" (Ps. 22:1). So did our Savior: "About three in the afternoon Jesus cried out in a loud voice . . . 'My God, my God, why have you forsaken me?'" (Matt. 27:46).

No shame exists in expressing our fears and doubts or in seeking God's answers to our questions in our place of desperation.

91

This process of lament was a robust part of the Hebrew culture, but one that we have lost in our twenty-first-century, Western worldview. We'll look at this process of lament more closely later. God desires our trust while we wait for him to answer. This is what the Hebrews lacked in their indictment of Moses and, by proxy, God. This trust is displayed when we simply keep waiting on God for an answer like a child who has asked their father for food. The child will wait expectantly for a response and will trust their father to provide, even if the initial response to the request is, "No, honey, it's not dinnertime yet." It's in the dark of night, when pain threatens to consume, that our attention is focused on God, and our relationship with him grows through that pleading sense of expectancy. Our faith grows in refusing to look elsewhere for our answers or satisfaction and in expectantly and patiently but steadfastly looking to our heavenly Father, the ultimate Problem Solver and authority in our lives, for his eventual, and eventually ultimate, provision. Our prayer remains, "Give us this day our daily bread" (Matt. 6:11 KJV), but also, "Thy kingdom come, Thy will be done" (v. 10 KJV).

> The questions we ask in the dark closet of pain attest to our need for God and our desire for relationship with him.

Greater Appreciation of God

Too often we desire God's explanation for his plan and his answer to why when he is more concerned with helping us relate to him on a deeper level through our suffering. When we're imprisoned by pain, at the end of our own strength, when striving on our own no longer suffices, we realize God never intended for us to try to make it on our own. Instead, God beckons us to go deeper in our relationship with him, to realize our dependence on him as we walk *through* the valley of pain and suffering.

Much of our pain experience provides a lesson in learning to live without being in control either of our circumstances or our destiny. When we look at Job and all the pain he endured, we see that despite his earnest pleas and desperation, God never answered his questions directly. Instead, God opened Job's eyes to a greater appreciation of God's power, majesty, and character.

Sometimes in our painful despair, we want one thing, such as physical healing, when God longs to offer infinitely more than we even realize we need. During my five months of medically prescribed bed rest, I wrestled with my worth. Previously a high achiever and a go-getter, I was unable to do much of anything. Nor could I be the doctor I was—the peg on which I hung my identity at the time. In that suffering, God taught me he loved me not for what I did but because of whose I was. If I never worked another day, he wouldn't love me less, and if I returned to work and continued to put one hundred hours a week into trying to save the world, he wouldn't love me more. That lesson was life altering and life giving and one I would have missed had I not endured the painful trial.

We Either Walk Away From or Toward God

The woman with the issue of blood exhibited great faith in believing that merely touching the threads on the bottom of Jesus's cloak would be sufficient to physically heal her. In studying her story, I contemplated what else Jesus offered her in that momentary exchange. She longed for physical healing, and Jesus offered her healing—comprehensive healing for her body, heart, mind, and soul.

Scripture says,

> Then the woman, seeing that she could not go unnoticed, came trembling and fell at his feet. In the presence of all the people, she told why she had touched him and how she had been instantly healed. Then he said to her, "Daughter, your faith has healed you. Go in peace." (Luke 8:47–48)

In that moment, not only did Jesus physically heal the woman, but he *saw* her, he *validated* her and her worth, he *offered* her a future, and he *gave* her a testimony, none of which she would have experienced simply in the absence of pain and suffering.

> Not only did Jesus physically heal the woman, but he *saw* her, he *validated* her and her worth, he *offered* her a future, and he *gave* her a testimony, none of which she would have experienced simply in the absence of pain and suffering.

Perhaps in our longing for healing, God is beckoning us to exercise our faith, to come to him and touch the hem of his garment regardless of who or how many are present, while continuing to believe and wait. Jesus repeatedly states throughout Scripture, "Come to me . . ." (e.g., Matt. 11:28; Luke 18:16). He still beckons today, and the choice is ours. Perhaps when we feel abandoned by God, we are the ones who are missing seeing him or who have walked away and need to look again or turn back to him.

Lessons on Healing

Healing often takes work. *Hard work.* Whether you experience physical illness, estranged relationships, emotional heartache, financial destitution, or some other pain, there is hope. Jesus asks, "Do you want to be made well?" (John 5:6 NKJV).

I treasure the story in John 5 regarding the lame man at Bethesda's pool. An angel of God frequented this pool, and Scripture says whoever stepped in first was healed from whatever disease ailed them. It then says,

> Now a certain man was there who had an infirmity thirty-eight years. When Jesus saw him lying there, and knew that he already had been in that condition a long time, He said to him, "Do you want to be made well?"
>
> The sick man answered Him, "Sir, I have no man to put me into the pool when the water is stirred up; but while I am coming, another steps down before me."
>
> Jesus said to him, "Rise, take up your bed and walk." And immediately the man was made well, took up his bed, and walked. (John 5:5–9 NKJV)

Since I am a neuropsychologist, people come to my office because something is wrong in their lives and they are seeking healing from what ails them. Early in my career, I thought it odd that Jesus asked the lame man, "Do you want to be made well?" I figured, of course he did . . . he was at the pool just waiting for someone to gently push him in so he could receive his healing. Over the last three decades, I've realized not everyone truly desires to get well. Some people are more comfortable in the known discomfort of their pain than they are in the unknown discomfort of healing. Some are afraid of the unknown. Some people come to the pool but just want to be seen in their sickness. Some have the routine figured out and don't want their world disrupted.

There are several important lessons from this passage in John 5:

1. **The lame man exhibited great faith.** Scripture says, "then whoever stepped in first, after the stirring of the

water, was made well of whatever disease he had" (v. 4 NKJV). The lame man couldn't step in by himself, but he exhibited great faith because *he stayed there waiting for his miracle.*

2. **The lame man never gave up hope.** He waited, ill for thirty-eight years, yet *he never gave up hope that he would be made well.*

    I don't know what pain you experience today. I don't know what you're praying for. But follow his example. He held on to hope for thirty-eight years. He didn't give up and was ultimately rewarded. Had he given up and ceased coming to the pool, he would've missed Jesus and not received his healing. *Even when the journey is long, never give up.*

3. **Jesus knew the man's condition, and he knows ours.** Scripture reveals that when Jesus saw the lame man lying there, he *knew* without being told that the man had been in that condition. Jesus didn't have to ask the doctors for the man's medical history. Jesus knew. *Jesus knows our condition as well. We don't have to tell him—he knows and he cares.*

    He knows our pain. He loves when we pray and share our needs, but he already knows. He knows you. He sees you. His heart breaks with yours. We often try to hide our pain from him. I did. I didn't want to lay my pain vulnerable before the Lord. Some pain, some things I was ashamed of, felt too messy to share with him. But eventually, my pain spilled out through my tearful cries. Then he whispered to my heart, *Finally you're talking to me about it. I've known all along; I was just waiting for you to approach me to talk about it.*

4. **We get to participate in our healing.** Jesus asked the man if he wanted to get well. We'd expect that he would have wanted to. But so often we don't really want to get well. Sometimes our journey to healing the pain requires medical attention or counseling. Other times it means getting a second job or giving up incidentals. In some situations, it requires either asking forgiveness or offering forgiveness, even when it isn't requested. Regardless of the type of pain, *the path to healing often requires some hard work on our part.*

5. **The lame man gave up a lot by doing the hard work.** In getting healed, he had to relinquish his identity as "the lame man." He would no longer be pitied. He would no longer be cared for. He would need to get a job and work for a living. He would have to make new friends, explain repeatedly to old friends, and endure the rejection of those who couldn't handle his healing. But then he also got to live his new, free identity in Christ. *There's always a risk in getting well, but the payoff is beautiful.*

6. **The lame man had to act first before healing came.** Jesus first told him to do something—specifically to get up, pick up his pallet, and walk—*then* he healed him. The lame man first exercised his faith in making the attempt to rise, balance, and walk—activities that had been beyond his conception for nearly four decades—but in looking beyond his history and trusting this oddly compelling stranger in front of him, he was rewarded and made well. *It's hard work sometimes, but God rewards obedience.*

97

Regardless of the pain you're suffering, hope prevails. But sometimes God calls us to do the hard heart work before we see the manifestation of our healing. Picking up and reading this book demonstrates your willingness to invest in your healing.

The Hem of His Garment

My suffering was good for me,
for it taught me to pay attention to your decrees.

Psalm 119:71 NLT

Your Rx

1. Unlike the Hebrews of Exodus, who didn't recognize God's provision in their suffering, ask God to reveal to you how he has provided for your needs throughout your pain journey.

2. Review the lessons above from the account of the lame man. Which aspect do you most need God's help with? Ask him for it.

3. Look up Psalms 3:3–5; 71:19–21; and 119:71. Write the verses on index cards and place them where you will see them frequently. Read these passages aloud three times daily, committing them to memory. Ask God to reveal himself to you in your pain.

My Prayer for You

Father, I thank you for leading your much-loved child to read these pages and for their opportunity to grow closer to you through their pain. Following Jesus's example, we cry out to you in our pain and suffering because we have nowhere else to turn. We know you are here with us and your will is better than ours. Please hold the one reading these words close because this is hard; we can't endure without you. Help this dear one to resist the temptation to walk away from you and to lean into you instead, for your Word says that if we draw near to you, you will draw near to us. We long for you to draw near, to hold us, to comfort us, to remind us that we aren't alone, and to teach us more about you through our pain filled journey. Help your child learn to relate to you in a more intimate way because of and despite their suffering. In Jesus's name, amen.

Recommended Playlist

"Thank You Jesus for the Cross," LIFE Worship, © 2021 by LIFE Worship

"Known, Seen, Loved," MŌRIAH, © 2021 by Cathedral Company

"DNA," Apollo LTD, © 2021 by Residence Music

"No One Ever Cared for Me Like Jesus," Steffany Gretzinger, © 2020 by Provident Label Group, LLC

7

Permission to Lament

My career had just started to accelerate after over a decade of training, my husband and I were enjoying raising our toddler son after years of waiting to start our family so I could finish my education, and we were settling into our new home in Texas when our sails fell limp as the wind was taken from our breath and our lives. My mother was diagnosed with advanced-stage lung cancer and was given a poor prognosis, and my husband was diagnosed with a rare form of abdominal cancer that necessitated a twenty-three-hour surgery with a one-in-four chance of survival.

Since my father died of a massive heart attack when I was a child, I had always feared something happening to my husband that would leave me a widow. As we sat across from the first oncologist we'd visited postdiagnosis, who literally used the phrase "Get your affairs in order" and offered a two-year prognosis, Job 3:25 resonated with me: "What I always feared has happened to me. What I dreaded has come true" (NLT).

During that stressful, painful time, I poured out my lament before the Lord like I'd never done before: "Father, my heart *hurts as I consider all our family is enduring, with a new career, a toddler to raise, and the uncertainty surrounding Mom's and Scott's diagnoses. I don't want to end up a widow like my mother did as a young bride, and I don't want our son to be fatherless. I know this didn't take you by surprise, and I know your purpose, plan, and timing are perfect even when we don't understand. I trust you, Lord, even when I do not see a way out, and I humbly ask you to embolden my faith for the journey where it is weak."*

What Is Lament?

When we review different types of prayer, we readily think of responsive or reflective prayers, which retrospectively express contentment, praise, or thanksgiving for God's provision. Another familiar form of prayer is that of supplication and intercession, which expresses a sense of expectation concurrent or synchronous in time with a circumstance. Prayers of lament, however, fall between those two categories. They express personal despair or loss and are couched within an appeal to the character and expected presence of God. They may or may not include an explicit statement of need. Prayers of lament are both contemporaneous with unresolved issues and reflective of prior experiences with God's presence, character, and provision.

To lament is to "feel, show, or express grief, sorrow, or regret, or to mourn deeply."[1] It is an honest and transparent statement of where we are when life is painful and tough. Expressions of lament can take the form of either words or actions and communicate anguish, disappointment, and at times even protest over an unwanted circumstance, yet the expression is not in the absence of faith. Job offered his lament to God verbally and behaviorally, tore his clothing, sat silently in ashes, and scraped his pain-racked body with broken pottery. God understands our human nature and our desire to wrap up our pain-prompted questions with a perfectly tied spiritual bow. Yet when we offer a heart of surrender instead of a demand for answers, he welcomes our heartfelt lament. The God who is present and who listens offers us lament as a gift to process our pain even in the absence of his interventions or the explanations we desire.

Prayers of lament frequently involve our cycling through crying out in anguish, sharing the painful problem we endure, prayerfully pleading for God's help, and having confidence in God's ability to meet our need. Lament stems from our times of grief, brokenheartedness, helplessness, or sinfulness. Lament offers comfort because it is voiced to a God who is present and who listens. It reflects hope because within it is a recognition of God's sovereign control and his eventual reconciliation or redemption of our heartache. The unique nature of lament, woefully lost in our culture even among Christians, balances our despair with a hope in the God who makes all things new.

The book of Lamentations expresses pain, grief, and horror on behalf of the Jewish people at the destruction of the temple and of the city of Jerusalem, the city of God's people and the place where he dwelled on earth. Its ruin was previously unthinkable to the Jewish people, and the reality of it confronted them with difficult questions of who they were, who God was, and what this catastrophe signified. The book provides an example for us of people who wrestled with God's ways, the ways that we often experience during our painful circumstances. As I recently pondered Lamentations, chapter 3 was crucial for helping me appreciate God's character: He is

> The unique nature of lament, woefully lost in our culture even among Christians, balances our despair with a hope in the God who makes all things new.

not only a just God but also a God of hope (vv. 21, 24–25), love and compassion (v. 22), faithfulness (v. 23), and salvation (v. 26).

Lament in Grief

Upon the death of Jairus's daughter in Luke 8, some people outside the residence were lamenting in their grief. "Meanwhile, all the people were wailing and mourning for her. 'Stop wailing,' Jesus said. 'She is not dead but asleep'" (v. 52). Similarly, Joseph, Pharaoh's officials, the senior officers of Egypt, and the senior members of Pharaoh's household lamented Jacob's death. "They lamented loudly and bitterly; and there Joseph observed a seven-day period of mourning for his father" (Gen. 50:10). Jeremiah 31:15 shares Rachel's lament: "A voice is heard in Ramah, mourning and great weeping, Rachel weeping for her children and refusing to be comforted, because they are no more."

Lament in Brokenheartedness

Psalm 130:1 reflects in lamentation a pervasive sense of brokenheartedness while also reflecting ultimate dependence on God's intervention: "Out of the depths I cry to you, LORD." Similarly, Psalm 102:1–2 is a prayer written by one who is overwhelmed with trouble and intent on pouring out his problems to the Lord:

> Hear my prayer, LORD!
> And let my cry for help come to You.
> Do not hide Your face from me on the day of my distress;
> Incline Your ear to me;
> On the day when I call answer me quickly. (NASB)

Lament in Helplessness

In 2 Chronicles 20:12, King Jehoshaphat laments his helplessness in the face of a large army coming against Israel and desperately seeks God's intervention: "Our God, will you not judge them? For we have no power to face this vast army that is attacking us. We do not know what to do, but our eyes are on you." In the angst he expresses to God, he pithily captures the overarching theme of lament: *"We do not know what to do, but our eyes are on you."*

Our times of lament are essentially expressions of our need for God's presence and intervention in our helpless, and at times seemingly hopeless, situations. "My soul is in deep anguish. How long, LORD, how long?" (Ps. 6:3). Perhaps some of our most heartfelt, honest expressions to God come within the context of lament that arises from life's pain-filled circumstances. God never shames us for our need for him. In fact, Jesus expressed lamentation to his Father as an example and a model to us when he cried out to God the night before he was crucified: "'*Abba*, Father,' he said, 'everything is possible for you. Take this cup from me. Yet not what I will, but what you will'" (Mark 14:36).

Lament over Sinfulness

We tend to consider lament as something only we do. But the Bible records examples of when God himself lamented both our creation ("The LORD regretted that he had made human beings on the earth, and his heart was deeply troubled" [Gen. 6:6]) and our sinful rebellion ("How often they rebelled against him in the wilderness and grieved him in the wasteland!" [Ps. 78:40]).

When we come to intimately know God and view our sinfulness the way he does, it produces in us lament over our sinful nature and an intent to turn away from sin and follow God's commands. "Godly sorrow brings repentance that leads to salvation and leaves no regret, but worldly sorrow brings death" (2 Cor. 7:10).

105

The Difference between Lament and Complaint

On occasion, I have heard that lament is just a fancied-up church version of complaint. Lament and complaint may appear similar, but upon closer inspection, they are distinctly different. Complaint says, "This is not fair to me." Lament says, "This is not fair to the character of God." God is not a God of evil or loss or pain or grief. His perfect creation did not include those things. They came later, after the fall. So, when evil or loss happens, it reflects something that is outside the expression of God's perfect character and is a slight to that character. In lament, we highlight the discontinuity between our present circumstances and the character of God. The circumstances we lament may be an affront to us, but they are a greater affront to God.

Lament is, in effect, an expression of the pain we experience but with a recognition of God's presence and an attitude of trust and hopeful expectation of God's eventual and providential intervention. Complaining is essentially having a self-focused pity party while we dwell on our pain. Complaining is expecting that God *should* do something for us. Lamenting is appealing to God's sovereignty, goodness, and mercy from a place of recognizing our own human frailty and sometimes our own participation in the difficult circumstances.

Creating Space for Lament

You can't heal from pain until you first feel it and honor it. Lament recognizes and gives a voice to pain, loss, suffering, and heartache. The Jewish tradition of sitting shivah validates lament.[2] Job and his friends sat shivah for a week as a behavioral expression of lament. As brothers and sisters in Christ, we need to honor the need of others to lament without judgment, correction, or Bible-verse Band-Aids like Job's friends offered.

Mary, Martha, and Lazarus were close friends of Jesus's, so the sisters' anguish and lament over Jesus's late arrival after Lazarus's illness, death, and burial is understandable. Yet hear Martha's confident expectation on the other side of grief: "'Lord,' Martha said to Jesus, 'if you had been here, my brother would not have died. But I know that even now God will give you whatever you ask'" (John 11:21–22). Mary echoes her sister's lamenting sentiment: "When Mary reached the place where Jesus was and saw him, she fell at his feet and said, 'Lord, if you had been here, my brother would not have died'" (v. 32).

Jesus entered his friends' grief and compassionately reflected our Father's care for us in our anguish when he joined his lament with that of Mary and Martha at their brother's tomb. Scripture tells us, "When Jesus saw [Mary] weeping, and the Jews who had come along with her also weeping, he was deeply moved in spirit and troubled" (v. 33) and that "Jesus wept" (v. 35). Then after Jesus went to the tomb and the stone was removed, "[he] looked up and said, 'Father, I thank you that you have heard me. I knew that you always hear me, but I said this for the benefit of the people standing here, that they may believe that you sent me'" (vv. 41–42).

Jesus knew that the purpose for his tarrying before arriving at Lazarus's tomb was greater than Mary and Martha could have fathomed when they lamented their brother's death. They would ultimately come to understand, but not before they literally laid their lament bare at his feet.

Our answers to why may not come this side of heaven, but in our pain, God welcomes our lament to set the stage for his love, compassion, and comfort in our suffering. Experiencing God's loving character always trumps understanding why we suffer, for it brings us closer to his heart and deepens our intimacy with him.

David was considered a man after God's own heart and struggled with some of the questions and feelings we do in our pain journeys. He wrestled with feeling abandoned by God in the depths of his pain, and cried out a lament partially repeated by Jesus on the cross:

> My God, my God, why have you forsaken me?
>   Why are you so far from saving me,
>   so far from my cries of anguish?
> My God, I cry out by day, but you do not answer,
>   by night, but I find no rest.
>
> Yet you are enthroned as the Holy One;
>   you are the one Israel praises. (Ps. 22:1–3)

The numerous examples in the Bible of those who offered prayers of lament indicate that not only is God willing to meet us where we are in the middle of our pain, but he is also interested in doing so. While God despises complaining, he welcomes lament because authentic lamentations spring from a recognition of his presence in our lives. They bring his children through a valley of suffering, onto a ridge of faith, down a road of hopeful petition, and up to a peak of praise.

Sadly, our Western culture decries that level of authenticity and vulnerability, including the time and effort it takes to find and name their pain. It is profoundly detrimental to a sufferer to deny such an honest expression of their pain. When we appreciate the intent of lament, we understand that even in the pain and "downs" of life, lament offers a chance to glorify God in the waiting and in the recognition that things are not as they should be. Lament expressed in God's presence reflects hope and assurance that resolution will ultimately come.

In Psalm 42, we read the author's desperation in verse two, his anguish in verse three, his declaration of praise despite his trial in verse four, and his honest angst and steadfast willingness to trust God through the trial in verse five:

> My soul thirsts for God, for the living God.
>   When can I go and meet with God?
> My tears have been my food
>   day and night,
> while people say to me all day long,
>   "Where is your God?"
> These things I remember
>   as I pour out my soul:
> how I used to go to the house of God
>   under the protection of the Mighty One
> with shouts of joy and praise
>   among the festive throng.
>
> Why, my soul, are you downcast?
>   Why so disturbed within me?
> Put your hope in God,
>   for I will yet praise him,
>   my Savior and my God. (Ps. 42:2–5)

Lament is a painful expression of grief and loss that lives between pain and sorrow on one end and trusting God's sovereignty on the other. Our lamentations will continue until the day Jesus returns.

The Gift of Lament

In our painful trials, God offers us the gift of lament as a place of brutal honesty regarding our pain and all its emotional baggage. And it is a gift. Even though lament is from our voice, it is offered in the presence of a listening and compassionate God. In our lament, he brings his presence to our pain. Lament offers a process of moving from an inward focus on our suffering to

109

an outward focus on who God is and all he is capable of. In the most terrible times of our lives, lament recognizes the continuing presence of God, and that, implicitly or explicitly, becomes praise. If we can step back from the pain for just a moment, we'll see that lament is the key to relinquishing control to God. For in lament, not only do we share the pain and hurt that we suffer, but we also offer our praise for who he is and for his sovereign control to work our pain for our good and his glory.

> In our lament, he brings his presence to our pain. Lament offers a process of moving from an inward focus on our suffering to an outward focus on who God is and all he is capable of.

Expressing lament reveals the tension between our pain and suffering and the hope-filled expectation we possess because of the sovereignty of God. We hurt, and yet we know God is our Healer. We suffer painful trials, and yet we know Jesus says he has overcome the world. We grieve over the depravity of the world while knowing that one day soon, Jesus will set right what is wrong and restore all that has been lost. Jesus understands our pain and suffering because he endured it himself. "He was despised and rejected by mankind, a man of suffering, and familiar with pain. Like one from whom people hide their faces he was despised, and we held him in low esteem" (Isa. 53:3).

Because of the cross, we can take comfort in knowing that we will suffer ("Dear friends, do not be surprised at the fiery ordeal that has come on you to test you, as though something strange were happening to you" [1 Peter 4:12]), that it will deepen our relationship to Jesus ("I want to know Christ—yes, to know the power of his resurrection and participation in his sufferings, becoming like him in his death" [Phil. 3:10]), but also that it is temporary ("For our light affliction, which is but for a moment, worketh for us a far more exceeding and eternal weight of glory" [2 Cor. 4:17 KJV]).

Please know that you aren't alone in your pain and heartache, and God wants you to pour out your heart to him. God is big enough to handle it. He is a safe place—he knows your pain anyway—but the Bible is the only book that has ever been written as an invitation from the author to get to know him and his love for you on a personal level. When we care about others, we want to know their hurts, their dreams, their struggles, and their victories, and that's how God feels about his children.

Perhaps we can take a lesson from our friend Job. After Job succumbs to the external pressure to blame God and to question why he would allow Job's suffering, God reveals his omniscience and power rather than answering Job's questions.

> Then Job replied to the LORD:
>
> > "I know that you can do anything,
> > and no one can stop you.
> > You asked, 'Who is this that questions my wisdom
> > with such ignorance?'
> > It is I—and I was talking about things I knew
> > nothing about,
> > things far too wonderful for me. . . .
> > I had only heard about you before,
> > but now I have seen you with my own eyes." (Job
> > 42:1–3, 5 NLT)

I encourage you not to despise the painful trials (hard, I know!) because they provide a new lens through which we see God. My prayer for you is that whatever pain you endure will give you new eyes to see our great and mighty God.

During sleepless, pain-filled nights, my thoughts often become prayers of lament. I admit my frailty, my need for God to intervene where I cannot, and my heartfelt desire to trust him in the waiting. I don't do it perfectly all the time, but I want to be obedient to God's call and commands more than I want to be comfortable. He calls us to pray about everything and to praise him and trust him, so that should be our habitual reaction. My pain-filled prayers of lament often sound something like this:

Father, this is hard. The pain is crushing and I long to be free from its vise grip. I know that you still heal today, and I ask that you take mercy on me and heal what is broken. But Lord, if you tarry in your answer, help me to learn the lessons you have for me in the hurting. Help me trust you not just when it's easy but also when it's hard. Help me trust you not just when it makes sense but also when I don't understand. I believe and praise you because you do work all things, including my painful trials, together for my good and for your glory. Show me your glory, Lord! In Jesus's name, amen.

The Hem of His Garment

A prayer of an afflicted person who has grown weak and pours out a lament before the LORD.

> Hear my prayer, LORD;
>   let my cry for help come to you.
> Do not hide your face from me
>   when I am in distress.
> Turn your ear to me;
>   when I call, answer me quickly.
>
>   Psalm 102:1–2

---------- **Your Rx** ----------

1. How does Jesus's example of praying a prayer of lament to his Father change or support your view of lament in your pain journey?

2. If you have not previously been accustomed to praying prayers of lament, how will you incorporate them into your pain journey now?

3. Look up Psalms 102:1–2; 42:2–5; and 1 Peter 4:12–13. Write the verses on index cards and place them where you will see them frequently. Read these passages aloud three times daily, committing them to memory. Ask God to reveal himself to you in your pain.

My Prayer for You

Father, I thank you that you never minimize our pain, but rather, you care so much for this dear one's hurting heart that you give them the gift of permission to lament. We come to you in deep and honest expression of our pain and anguish. We know none of this takes you by surprise. While we long for you to remove it from our lives, we recognize that your plan, your way, and your timing are all perfect, and we trust you in them, knowing that you never waste our pain. We surrender our desires and our ways to you, knowing that you are good and that you are incapable of anything but good. You are holy and perfect, and we offer our praise for who you are in our lives. Help us to reflect your life and light in all we say and do. In Jesus's name, amen.

Recommended Playlist

"Still in Control," Mack Brock, © 2017 by Sparrow Records; Capitol CMG, Inc.

"Meet Me There," Lydia Laird, © 2020 by Provident Label Group, LLC

"SOS," We the Kingdom, © 2019 by Sparrow Records; Capitol CMG, Inc.

"The Garden," Kari Jobe, © 2017 by KAJE, LLC

8

Coping with God's Silence

*"I'm tired of praying when it doesn't seem to make a differ-
ence. I can honestly say I can't think of a single prayer God has
answered for me in the past year," I sincerely bemoaned to a
close friend. I continued: "Why continue to pray when it makes
no difference? I'm not like you—I'm not a prayer warrior. The
pain hurts so bad, I just need to know God cares." I hated to
be so honest with what I deemed to be my spiritual failings,
but the pain robbed me of the energy to maintain a spiritual
façade. "Praying and not seeing him work to heal or alleviate
my pain leaves me feeling abandoned by the One who promises
never to leave or abandon us."*

*More than once I lamented to praying friends, "I just don't
understand what God is doing or why he doesn't intervene and
provide." And yet, I think of the times Job cried out to God,
almost demanding an answer. God never directly answered
Job's question, but he did reveal more of himself, and for that
Job ultimately expressed gratitude.*

A Universal Struggle

God's silence is more difficult to understand and accept than any other experience we have with him. In our pain, this silence can feel excruciating, and it can threaten to tip us into despair or desperation and prompt a sense of rejection or abandonment by God.

Have you ever felt defeated or like you didn't possess God's favor when your prayers didn't bring the answers you desired? Perhaps you've tried to craft answers to your prayers yourself when at best it seemed God wasn't answering and at worst like he was being silent. *What do you do when you've prayed, risked the perceived embarrassment and humiliation of sharing the real and raw, and laid your pain before him, yet you don't find answers?* I think that is one of the greatest challenges in the pain journey: feeling unseen and uncared for while you attempt to hold on to hope that your pain will be healed.

> I think that is one of the greatest challenges in the pain journey: feeling unseen and uncared for while you attempt to hold on to hope that your pain will be healed.

Honestly, in those times when the pain's scream is deafening and I'm not sure I can take another breath—or that I even want to—I pray, I cry, I grieve, I lament. I tell God where I'm struggling, and I ask for strength and persistence as I try to patiently wait for his answer. It's hard to live in the tension between "God asks us to pray for healing" and "Where is God and where is the healing?" Holding that tension is heavy and seems interminable at times, especially when the weight of pain is crushing.

116

God in the Dark

Why does God seem silent in our suffering? That is an ancient conundrum. People have asked and attempted to answer this question since the days of Adam and Eve. The most simple and honest answer is that we don't know why God is sometimes silent or why he allows suffering to continue. As creatures, we aren't always privy to the why of our Creator. Paul alludes to this in 1 Corinthians 2:11 when he states that "no one knows the thoughts of God except the Spirit of God." Then in 2 Corinthians 12, Paul describes his repeated pleading with God to remove what he calls the thorn in his flesh (v. 7).

God is God, and we are not. During our painful times when God seems silent or distant, our experience with him is not definitive and doesn't emotionally satisfy. But even lacking a definitive and emotionally satisfying explanation, we can garner some perspective. We may experience dark nights, but God has not left us alone and he has provided some illumination, which persists even in our suffering and through his silence.

Before we get to that, let me ask another question: Would you *really* feel better if you knew the why of your pain, if God answered your query? Would your pain lessen if you discovered a noble cause for the suffering? Methinks the pain would still exist just as intensely, even if the why satisfied our hearts. Knowing the reason for pain doesn't eliminate it. Intellectual satisfaction doesn't dull pain's presence. Is it possible that in the persistence of the pain we would simply change our questioning? Instead of asking why, would we ask God to achieve this noble purpose another way so that our pain could be removed? It is possible that knowing why might worsen the pain or provoke bitterness if we disliked what we heard. If we had an answer, would we be more likely to argue or not accept God's response? If God responded to our current situation, would we

117

automatically expect an equal response during our next painful experience or during a friend's latest struggle? Is it really fair to expect God to answer us? Is it even useful to have an answer?

Heard, Seen, Recognized, and Valued

God isn't absent from our pain, even if we don't have the answers or resolutions we'd like, and even if we perceive silence from him. Pain grabs our attention and colors our perspective. It presents as "in our face" and creates an obstacle to look past. It makes us more internally focused. It blots out the rest of life, darkening our ability to see or understand the people and the world around us.

Periods of unbearable pain dominate phases of our lives. The pain's discordant melody grates and rasps, and with every hour or day its presence grows in our lives, like the off-key violin whose spotlighted solo obscures everything else happening onstage. Everything in life is perceived through the lens of pain. That lens, which distorts our earthly relationships and experiences, also diminishes our perception of God and our ability to see his hand or hear his voice. Yet just as the symphony isn't only about the violin's solo, life isn't all about pain. Other things are happening.

These other things include, most significantly, God's offer of his own presence and attentiveness. Isaiah 41:10 tells us, "Do not fear, for I am with you; do not be dismayed, for I am your God." Two chapters later, we read, "When you pass through the waters, I will be with you" (43:2). God promises to be present with us, especially in times of trouble. Just a verse before this, God declares to his people, "Do not fear, for I have redeemed you; I have summoned you by name; you are mine" (v. 1). God is attentive to his children. He brings each of us to him. God knows each of our names. First Peter 3:12 gives us this: "For the

118

eyes of the Lord are on the righteous and his ears are attentive to their prayer." God listens.

God is present. God knows our name. God draws us to himself. God listens. As much as we want the pain of our current situation to end, we also want—even if we don't state or recognize it—someone to listen, to be present and attentive, and to recognize who we are. Dignity is conferred by the act of stopping, looking at the speaker, recognizing them, and listening to their expression of pain. And like a mother comforting an injured child, what a bonus if the person listening draws us to them and shares their comfort with us!

> Everything in life is perceived through the lens of pain. That lens, which distorts our earthly relationships and experiences, also diminishes our perception of God and our ability to see his hand or hear his voice.

As a young child, I dimly recall becoming separated from my parents on a shopping trip and getting lost in a department store. My vague memory is imbued with a sense of panic and a realization that none of the strangers around me knew who I was nor did they know the urgency of my situation. I looked in all directions and could find nothing offering comfort, safety, or familiarity. That moment of lostness seemed to last for hours but could not have been more than seconds or minutes. Eventually I heard my name, and I recognized the voice. In an instant I went from being panicked and distraught to comforted and quiet. My parents reunited with me. They knew my name and my situation. They drew me to them. They heard me, saw me, recognized me, and comforted me.

Isn't this what we desire most? To be heard, seen, recognized, valued, and comforted? The teenager getting affirmation from the presence and attention of their current crush experiences a (temporary) sense of peace and comfort. Their world is right for the time. The young professional praised for their diligent and insightful efforts and brought into the circle of those whose attention they value finds a sense of harmony in their professional environment. Isn't a time of pain eased by a friend who remains truly present, attentive, and compassionate? But doesn't pain make it harder to recognize the gift of presence and attention offered by a friend? Don't we tend to become gripped by our loss, pain, or discomfort and miss the quiet presence of an attendant and attentive friend? Aren't we more tempted to decline a social invitation and diminish the possibility and value of connection or companionable time together when we are in the depths of pain?

God's Compassion

It's hard to hear God's voice when our pain deafens us to any input around us. And we can't expect those around us to speak louder or act more forcefully to help break through our isolation. When a teenager comes home in tears because of a slight from their crush, does their mom or dad grab their shoulders and look them sternly in the eye with an admonition to "buck up"? No. The parent sits the child down and listens, putting aside their phone or pressing household task. They may offer a soothing word or a hug in there somewhere, but the teen may not recognize it or even remember it the next day. The child is affirmed and comforted by the presence and attention of their parent even if the child does not perceive it. How much is this like our experience with God during our pain?

You may say, "I never had a compassionate parent. I never knew this experience you describe." That hurts my heart for you, but we have a God who *is* compassionate. These gifts from God—his presence and attentiveness, his recognition of each of us by name, his drawing of us to him, and his comfort—are marks of his character. He cannot be any other way toward his children. The apostle Paul tells us that God is "the Father of compassion and the God of all comfort, who comforts us in all our troubles" (2 Cor. 1:3–4). If there is compassion or comfort, God is present, even if we don't perceive it.

God's presence and attention are not the only things he offered us for this life or the painful situations we encounter. To the Philippians, Paul describes a peace beyond understanding that comes from continuing to engage with the God of presence, attentiveness, and comfort (see Phil. 4:6–7). The writer of Hebrews encourages us to "approach God's throne of grace with confidence, so that we may receive mercy and find grace to help us in our time of need" (4:16). We have the privilege of coming to God on our timetable. We aren't required to wait for a summons from the King. Two in the morning? Fine. Middle of a staff meeting? Fine. At the hospital in angst and despair? Fine.

We may not hear a definitive response from God regarding our situation or our pain. Our pain might obscure our sense of God's presence. But that doesn't mean he is absent, and that doesn't mean he is not working or speaking to us or into our lives.

The Hem of His Garment

Therefore we do not lose heart. Though outwardly we are wasting away, yet inwardly we are being renewed day by day. For our light and momentary troubles are achieving for us an eternal glory that far outweighs them all. So we fix our eyes not on what is seen, but on what is unseen, since what is seen is temporary, but what is unseen is eternal.

2 Corinthians 4:16–18

Your Rx

1. We've probably all struggled with times when God seemed silent. Prayerfully ask God to reveal to you the lies you believed during those silent periods as well as his truth to refute the lies.

2. Prayerfully ask God to remind you of times when you experienced both his presence and his compassion, then record those instances in a place you can refer to when you need encouragement in the future.

3. Look up Isaiah 43:2–3; 1 Peter 3:12; and 2 Corinthians 1:3–5. Write the verses on index cards and place them where you will see them frequently. Read these passages aloud three times daily, committing them to memory. Ask God to reveal himself to you in your pain.

My Prayer for You

Father, you are sovereign, and you are good. Your mercies to us are new each morning. Lord, you are our Provider, and the lifter of our heads. We trust that you know what we need and what we don't, even when we don't understand or agree. I know you love this reader dearly and care about their pain. Help them to trust your goodness toward them and to be thankful for your protection and guidance. Your Word promises that those who trust in you will not be disappointed. Today we choose to trust you, Lord. In Jesus's name, amen.

Recommended Playlist

"God of All My Days," Casting Crowns, © 2016 by Provident Label Group, LLC

"Trust in You," Lauren Daigle, © 2015 by Centricity Music

"Breakthrough Miracle Power," Passion and Maverick City, © 2021 by Capitol CMG, Inc.

"Call On Your Name," Elle Limebear, © 2021 by Provident Label Group, LLC

9

Waiting on God

The radiation technician's smile comforted me as I lay down on the cold, hard "bed." She calmly explained each step of the procedure. She didn't know my professional background or that I knew the intricacies of this procedure. Nor did she know that I needed the assurance as a patient rather than as a doctor that day. "I'm going to leave you, but I'll be able to hear you from behind the wall if you need anything." I realized I had already been holding my breath for what seemed like days. Ever since my doctor informed me, "We need to run a few more tests to get a better idea of what's causing your pain," I'd begun holding it a little longer . . . waiting.

Immediately after she left my side, I felt alone in that large, sterile room. Alone, but not really. God promised never to leave me. I knew that, but my soul longed to feel it too. I closed my eyes and tried to think of anything except the several diagnoses we were trying to rule out through this procedure. There was nothing inviting about the cold, hard, clinical table. The paper "sheet" crinkled as I moved into the scanner. The robotic instructions bellowed, "Breathe . . . Hold. Your. Breath."

I anxiously awaited a diagnosis and treatment plan. But I didn't need to. Whatever the diagnosis, God and I would face it together. He cautioned, "Be still, and know that I am God" (Ps. 46:10). The scan would (hopefully) identify any physical abnormality contributing to my pain and discomfort, yet God already knew my condition, and he saw the attitude of my heart. Even modern medicine wasn't that good.

More than a diagnosis, treatment, and cure, I desired a closer relationship with the Lord and stronger faith. If God chose to use this experience toward that end, then it was serving a larger purpose. The uncertainty ushered in anxious thoughts, which

The fruit that grows in the valley of trials is rich.

I intentionally took captive, remembering God hadn't given me a spirit of fear, but of power, love, and a sound mind (see 2 Tim. 1:7 NKJV). I repented for agreeing with the spirit of fear and accepted God's peace. Nothing about my circumstances surprised God, nor were they too big for him to manage.

Pain continually reminded me something offensive and hostile existed within my body. More importantly, I didn't want anything offensive within my heart that didn't belong there or that pained my heavenly Father.

After the procedure, the technician advised, "Drink lots of water today." I considered that instruction throughout the day because I most desired an infusion of Jesus's living water. We all experience pain, and I admitted to a friend that I didn't want this pain but that if I had to experience it, I wanted to learn whatever God had for me to learn in and through it. I wanted to really try to count it all joy, for the fruit that grows in the valley of trials is rich.

While I looked to doctors to diagnose and treat what ailed me, I looked to God and waited on him to search not just my physical body but also the condition of my heart and to heal whatever he identified to be other than the way he created it so that I could be restored in his sight.

He is Jehovah Rapha, the God who heals.

Coping While Waiting for God to Heal

Scripture tells us that what we invest in, or sow, is what we will harvest. Sowing is a principle of God's kingdom that means to do the work needed in advance of a result, but it is also used to describe a farmer planting seed in hopes of a harvest.

Before the age of mechanization, a farmer would scatter seed by hand. He would walk back and forth across his land, taking a step and throwing seed, then taking another step and throwing more seed. It was simple and repetitive. It took no elaborate tools or superhuman effort. The farmer expected no immediate response or reward for his efforts and would have been unprepared to harvest a crop if it had magically sprung up as he sowed. He would cast the seed and keep walking. But the farmer knew that those minimal efforts would result in a harvest sometime in the future.

The principle of sowing is useful as we walk through pain. Pain sufferers know that sometimes life becomes compressed to the point of just taking the next breath, of taking another step. But even within this compressed scope, sowing is possible. Even as pain blots out everything else in life and limits our attention to just the next moment, we can still sow the seeds of relationship with this God who we know is present, attentive, and available and who calls us by name and to himself. This sowing may not result in the relief from pain we so longingly seek, but it may offer a way to push back the blinding blot of pain that robs us of the experience of life and keeps us chained to just the next step and the next moment. Here are some ways to sow that might help push back the pain.

Keep Praying Honestly

God isn't afraid of our honest requests—he knows them anyway. But sometimes he wants to see if we're willing to share our vulnerability with him. Just as parents long to hear from their children once they've left the nest, God wants to hear from his children. Jesus tells us, "Ask and it will be given to you; seek and you will find; knock and the door will be opened to you. For everyone who asks receives; the one who seeks finds; and to the one who knocks, the door will be opened" (Matt. 7:7–8). Don't focus only on praying for relief from your pain, although it might be tempting. Praying for relief is appropriate, but focusing only on that intense and immediate desire will rob you of the greater benefit of seeking God's presence in your situation and in the larger part of your life. Ask God to walk with you through your pain journey. Ask him to show you his presence within your situation. Share your thoughts and feelings about your pain with him. Let him (and yourself) hear your lament verbally. Speak your frustrations and grief. List your losses. Don't try to sanitize your prayer because you think God only wants to hear churchy or spiritual-sounding prayer. Be honest with him—and yourself.

We read in 1 Thessalonians 5:17 Paul's directive to "pray continually," while 1 Chronicles 16:11 tells us, "Seek the LORD and his strength; seek his presence continually!" (ESV). God already knows what we think and what we need, but continually praying and sharing our concerns keeps our focus on God and keeps us in relationship with him.

How many times have you brought up a topic again that you've previously talked about with a friend? Why? Because it's important to you, and you need a safe place to share. God is that safe place. "Because he bends down to listen, I will pray as long as I have breath!" (Ps. 116:2 NLT).

Read the Prayers of Others Who Have Endured Pain

Sometimes our pain seems too great to construct a prayer, even silently. In these times and others, we can read or listen to the prayers of other people who have walked that path before us. The book of Psalms is a great place to start with this since so many of the psalms are expressed as prayers. The writers of these psalms are authentic in their description of life's difficulties. They voice loss, grief, fear, shame, physical pain, weakness, and frailty. Read through the psalms until you find one that resonates. Then read it again slowly, a verse or two at a time, pausing to consider the words and the topic. Listen to what the writer is saying. Look through the poetic structure and see the travail of the human who is speaking and the presence of the God who is listening. Often, psalms will include both a lament, or an expression of grief or loss, and a response. They can be useful to see how other sufferers expressed their pain and then how they responded to it.

Ask in Jesus's Name and Follow His Example

There is power in Jesus's name, in his blood, and in his resurrection. He told us to pray using his name, with the ultimate outcome being great joy. "You haven't done this before. Ask, using my name, and you will receive, and you will have abundant joy" (John 16:24 NLT). But the name of Jesus isn't some magical code that we utter to unlock a result we seek. In Scripture, names often referred to a person's character or disposition. Praying in Jesus's name means to pray in a way that is consistent with who Jesus is and with his purpose. Jesus gave us a model for how to pray in Matthew 6:5–15, and this model reflects his character and priorities. The interesting thing about the Lord's Prayer is that it does not involve asking for but rather declaring a reality greater than our earthly one, aligning ourselves with God's will over our own—on earth as it is in heaven. When we prioritize God's will over our earthly wishes, our delight in the answer mirrors God's delight.

Pray Believing God Will Answer

Sometimes, when pain consumes us and we come to the end of ourselves, we throw up a Hail Mary prayer, hoping God will answer. But in the back of our mind, we are wondering if he really will or if he even cares. That's not the kind of prayer God honors. Scripture is clear that when we pray, we must do so believing God will answer. He is looking for a heart of faith and a willingness to trust and believe before we see the result. "But when you ask, you must believe and not doubt, because the one who doubts is like a wave of the sea, blown and tossed by the wind. That person should not expect to receive anything from the Lord. Such a person is double-minded and unstable in all they do" (James 1:6–8).

Believing that God will answer our prayers includes the idea that God may answer in a different way, time, or scope than what we consider ideal. Believing God will answer also includes the mandate to persist in seeking the answer. How often have I prayed about something I considered to be serious but then failed to come back to that prayer again or even to look for answers to my prayers?

We hold close the things that are important to us: We remember where we keep a valuable piece of jewelry or important paperwork, what the deadline is for significant tasks, when and where to meet a friend for coffee or lunch. Prayers about significant things, including our pain, fall into the same category. Remember how you spoke to God about your pain and what you asked him about or for. Bring it up again with him. He won't be bored or mad. He cares even more about an answer to your pain than you do. Talk about your pain with him in different ways. This can include talking to him about your memories, hopes, and fears, the details and progression of your pain experience, changes in your perspective on your situation, your thankfulness for resources or friends he has provided, and so on. You can also ask God to show his various characteristics or attributes to you in your situation. It is often hard to see God's goodness or gentleness or love in the midst of pain, so tell him you can't see it and ask him to show you where it is. Ask him to broaden your view of how you see your situation and your pain, and ask him to show you how he is answering your prayer. Then look for the beginnings of an answer or for indications of multiple answers in different areas or aspects of your life. You may be surprised by what you find.

Thank God

When we're in the waiting room, anticipating God's answer to our prayers, time seems to stretch to unimaginable lengths. When our focus is on God healing our pain, we often lose sight of all the ways he has already answered our other prayers. Focusing on God's prior faithfulness in my life keeps my heart tender and grateful and reminds me that God has been faithful before—even when I'm waiting for his answers now.

Scripture tells us that it is impossible to please God without faith. In our desire to experience God move on our behalf, it's important to thank him not only for what he has done in the past but also for what he is already doing that we cannot yet see. King Jehoshaphat employed a similar strategy when he was faced with attacks from three different enemy armies. Jehoshaphat possessed a solid faith and demonstrated it to the people.

After consulting the people, Jehoshaphat appointed men to sing to the LORD and to praise him for the splendor of his holiness as they went out at the head of the army, saying:

> "Give thanks to the LORD,
>   for his love endures forever." (2 Chron. 20:21)

When we exercise prayer and praise as tools in our battle arsenal, we voice our faith. No faith is required to thank God after he has answered our prayers, but true faith is exercised when we thank him before he answers. Jehoshaphat's army won the battle not through a physical fight but by exercising their faith in the One who could fight on their behalf. "As they began to sing and praise, the LORD set ambushes against the men of Ammon and Moab and Mount Seir who were invading Judah, and they were defeated" (2 Chron. 20:22).

Remember God Is Never Late

I don't know how many times in my life I've been impatient because I've wanted something to happen or for God to answer prayers on my timeline. Patience isn't one of my strengths, whether we're talking about gardening or waiting for God to answer my prayers. Throughout difficult circumstances, I've realized that God is always an "on-time God." He rarely answers prayers early, but he is also never late. His plan and his timing are perfect, and they are for our good.

Seek Greater Wisdom

When I'm tempted to think God is not answering my prayers, it's possible that my prayers may not align with his will for my life. Then I must ask for the wisdom to see his will for my life and the strength to accept it. "When you ask, you do not receive, because you ask with wrong motives, that you may spend what you get on your pleasures" (James 4:3). It's important to

132

remember that God's answer to our prayers may not be what we want but is most assuredly what we need. Frequently the answer to our prayers is a changing of our heart so that we become more like Christ and our desires align with God's. Sometimes we need to seek God's wisdom more than an abolishment of our pain. "If any of you lacks wisdom, you should ask God, who gives generously to all without finding fault, and it will be given to you" (James 1:5).

Stop and Reevaluate

Certain things can hinder God's answering our prayers, and it's prudent to stop and evaluate our situation and check our heart to see if our own behavior could be hindering God from answering our prayers.

Sin is one of the biggest hindrances to our prayers being answered. "It's your sins that have cut you off from God. Because of your sins, he has turned away and will not listen anymore" (Isa. 59:2 NLT). Fortunately, God wants to restore our relationship with him, so he provides the gift of confession and repentance to do so. "If my people, who are called by my name, will humble themselves and pray and seek my face and turn from their wicked ways, then I will hear from heaven, and I will forgive their sin and will heal their land" (2 Chron. 7:14). James parallels this when he says, "Come near to God and he will come near to you. Wash your hands, you sinners, and purify your hearts, you double-minded" (James 4:8).

Humility before God opens our eyes. It helps us to put aside our sense of ourselves and understand again that we are not yet brought to perfection. Pain and embarrassment may follow when we recognize within ourselves something that ought not be there, and it can be frustrating to become aware of something that is hindering our relationship with God. Not dealing with these things as the Holy Spirit shows them to us is a sure way not to see past our current situation and to continue to be frustrated and stuck where we are.

Trust God's Character

Physical, mental, emotional, relational, spiritual, and financial pain can all leave us feeling like we're stuck in a tornado, waiting to be flung into an unknown land, broken and scarred. During those times, when people and situations change constantly, it comforts me to remember that God is immutable; he never changes. God declares in Malachi 3:6, "I the LORD do not change." God never changes his will, his mind, or his nature. "Every good and perfect gift is from above, coming down from the Father of the heavenly lights, who does not change like shifting shadows" (James 1:17). Our confidence in ourselves, our situations, and our abilities is precarious, whereas we can rest our confidence in a God who never changes. "He who is the Glory of Israel does not lie or change his mind; for he is not a human being, that he should change his mind" (1 Sam. 15:29).

God's faithfulness is one of his character traits that we hold on to when our pain-filled storms whip and sling us against life's boulders. He meets our lament with his faithfulness, which encourages us as we wait for his answer to our desperate pleas.

> Because of the LORD's great love we are not consumed,
>   for his compassions never fail.
> They are new every morning;
>   great is your faithfulness.
> I say to myself, "The LORD is my portion;
>   therefore I will wait for him." (Lam. 3:22–24)

Deuteronomy 7:9 reminds us of God's faithfulness to those who obey him: "Know therefore that the LORD your God is God; he is the faithful God, keeping his covenant of love to

134

a thousand generations of those who love him and keep his commandments."

When we recognize God as our loving Father and the fact that he is good and incapable of anything but good, then trusting God's character helps us wait not only for his good and perfect plan for our lives but also for his good and perfect timing. God never withholds anything good from his children. "For the LORD God is a sun and shield; the LORD bestows favor and honor; no good thing does he withhold from those whose walk is blameless" (Ps. 84:11).

Knowing God's character, trusting his Word, and believing him to be our source of help puts us in the perfect posture for waiting on his answers. "God is our refuge and strength, an ever-present help in trouble" (Ps. 46:1). During painful, uncertain times, when situations are not as we had hoped, we must stay anchored to the reality of God's character. He warned that we would experience trials, and yet he offered the provision of his peace *despite* the circumstances: "I have told you these things, so that in me you may have peace. In this world you will have trouble. But take heart! I have overcome the world" (John 16:33).

Focus on God's Sovereignty

Regardless of how we suffer in this life, we must appreciate God's sovereignty. God isn't compelled to answer all our prayers, nor are we promised that he answers every prayer. Scripture assures us, "This is the confidence we have in approaching God: that if we ask anything according to his will, he *hears* us" (1 John 5:14, emphasis added). God knows and is aware of our need. He is not oblivious to, dismissive of, or insensitive to our troubles. We also read, "If you, then, though you are evil, know how to give good gifts to your children, how much more will your Father in heaven give good gifts to those

135

who ask him!" (Matt. 7:11). As we saw in the last chapter, God meets our needs. He listens and we have access to him. He is good and gives us good gifts. They just may be something other than what we seek in the moment.

Jesus understood and experienced this. His prayer in the garden of Gethsemane confirms that he sought relief from what was before him the night of his crucifixion.

> He took Peter, James and John along with him, and he began to be deeply distressed and troubled. "My soul is overwhelmed with sorrow to the point of death," he said to them. "Stay here and keep watch."
>
> Going a little farther, he fell to the ground and prayed that if possible the hour might pass from him. "*Abba*, Father," he said, "everything is possible for you. Take this cup from me. Yet not what I will, but what you will." (Mark 14:33–36)

Christ's prayer in the garden is our example: Jesus endured incredible pain and essentially told God, "Father, I want you to take this pain away, but I want what you want more than I want to be rid of this pain." God tells us to ask, but then we surrender to God's sovereign will. We abide in peace and trust—not in the assurance or promise that our petition will be granted but in the peace of Christ himself. He is enough.

Praise Him

God lives within the presence of our praises. "But thou art holy, O thou that inhabitest the praises of Israel" (Ps. 22:3 KJV). Praising God despite difficult and painful situations is the kind of gift or sacrifice that pleases God. "Through Jesus, therefore, let us continually offer to God a sacrifice of praise—the fruit of lips that openly profess his name" (Heb. 13:15). In seasons of crushing pain, when we're tempted to feel anything but grateful and we perhaps struggle to keep our focus on God, our praise truly is a sacrifice as we choose to offer praise when we may be otherwise tempted to grumble and complain.

In seeking healing from our pain, we need to be more focused on the Healer than the healing. "Rejoice always, pray continually, give thanks in all circumstances; for this is God's will for you in Christ Jesus" (1 Thess. 5:16–18). It's easy to praise God when walking through life's green pastures. Our praise in life's painful storms requires faith. When our focus even in pain is on praise, prayer, and gratitude, our suffering, along with the praise, prayer, and gratitude, gives God glory.

> In seeking healing from our pain, we need to be more focused on the Healer than the healing.

Consider the Lessons

I've learned that God is more interested in our obedience than our comfort. He remains continuously at work teaching us, training us, and transforming us to reflect him to a lost and dying world. As we're seeking him and waiting for his answers, God is always teaching us lessons in our circumstances if we will have ears to hear and eyes to see. It's important to consider that when God doesn't answer our prayers as we hope he will, perhaps he is protecting us from something we wouldn't otherwise be aware of while preparing us for a better yes. "Yes, my soul, find rest in God; my hope comes from him" (Ps. 62:5).

In those circumstances when perseverance is required in prayer, perhaps the greatest gift is learning that we really aren't alone in our suffering and God is with us as he promises. We often won't understand why things happen. His ways are frequently not our ways. Yet we can be thankful and recognize that God never withholds what is good from his children.

We may never know why things happen as they do. But we can always know and trust that God will do what is in his character, which is good and abundant, and in his time, often protecting us from unseen harm.

The Hem of His Garment

Oh Lord, I cry out to you.
I will keep on pleading day by day.
Psalm 88:13 NLT

Your Rx

1. Some coping mechanisms represent habitual responses to pain and crises while others reflect a greater need for intentionality. Reread the suggestions for ways to cope while we wait on God to answer our prayers and heal our pain. Pick two or three to intentionally pursue in your current pain journey.

2. Consider the character traits of God. Select two or three that encourage you most in your current pain journey. Look up and record a Scripture or two about those traits as reminders on the more painful days when your memory is short.

3. Look up 2 Chronicles 7:14; Lamentations 3:22–24; and Psalm 84:11. Write the verses on index cards and place them where you will see them frequently. Read these passages aloud three times daily, committing them to memory. Ask God to reveal himself to you in your pain.

My Prayer for You

Father, I pray for the one reading these words right now. You know the pain they endure. I ask that you be faithful to your Word, comfort them in the dark and challenging places, and draw them into the secret place to spend time with you and to seek your will and your way. I thank you that you are already there in the secret place, waiting for each of us. Thank you in advance for your provision. In Jesus's name, amen.

Recommended Playlist

"Battle Belongs," Phil Wickham, © 2020 by Phil Wickham

"Waiting Here for You," Christy Nockels, © 2011 by six-stepsrecords/Sparrow Records

"Praise Is a Weapon," Mark & Sarah Tillman, © 2021 by Mark & Sarah Tillman

"You Already Know," JJ Heller, © 2020 by Stone Table Records

10

Voices from the Depths of Pain

Recently, on a particularly vulnerable day when my pain was relentless, I hesitantly shared a post (complete with tears) on social media. It was to the tune of "I'll Find You" by Lecrae, to which I added my thoughts: "Do you ever feel like you can't hold on any longer? Hold on just a little tighter, my friend. Like the woman with the issue of blood who knew she would be well if she could just reach the hem of Jesus's garment. Reach for his hem . . . he'll meet you there." Within moments, comments poured in faster and more frequently than on any of my typical posts. Clearly it had resonated with others who walked a painful journey. One particular reader noted, "Your words have brought me from the darkest places. I'm so thankful the Lord uses you to speak to the brokenhearted." Another commented, "Reach for the hem, Michelle. Our world needs you just a bit longer."

In all transparency, my heart's greatest desire is to share the comfort God has given me with those who are hurting and who are perhaps just a few steps behind me in their journey. But there have been a few occasions when I've bemoaned to the Lord, "Who is going to help me? I need help, I need encouragement, I need healing." Soon after, God spoke to my spirit and reminded me that he has provided many before us, in his written Word, to teach us, to help us, to encourage us, and whose words might even heal parts in us.

Overcoming Painful Times with Our Testimony

Has something ever happened that just rocked your world or took out your legs from beneath you? I experienced that when the doctor called unexpectedly to say, "I'm sorry to tell you this, but you have cancer." I sat stunned for a few seconds before she broke into my wildly running thoughts to ask if we could schedule surgery. I couldn't think clearly, much less talk on the phone and look at my calendar at the same time. I agreed to call back later. The next twenty-four hours were a whirlwind of emotions. Her words seemed unbelievable as I remained in shock for many hours. I believed I was healthy and reasonably physically fit.

As I shared the news with my closest friends and family, the shock waned, and the reality of the situation sunk in. Many had questions I couldn't answer or advice I didn't desire. But most offered to pray. And as I thanked each of them for their prayers, I also reiterated my faith in the Great Physician, to encourage them but also to bolster my own faith.

I appreciated that this hadn't taken God by surprise, and he already knew his plan to see me through whatever the future held. God had demonstrated his faithfulness repeatedly in my life, and I refused to doubt his faithfulness now.

Scripture declares that we defeat the enemy by the blood of the lamb and the word of our testimony (Rev. 12:11). Sharing our testimony of God's intervention in our life encourages others to trust him and to recognize their own testimonies of his work in their lives. It bolsters their faith when they need it. God uses our trials to build our faith, draw us closer to him, and give us a testimony of his faithfulness for others to see.

> God uses our trials to build our faith, draw us closer to him, and give us a testimony of his faithfulness for others to see.

As I reflected on what this health journey held for me, I turned to Scripture to build my faith. I'm thankful God gave us the Bible to guide us, to encourage us, to comfort us. In painful times, I remember God's care for his people in Scripture.

Take Encouragement and Comfort from Testimonies in Scripture

If you're wondering why God isn't answering your heart-wrenching questions in the depths of your despair, you're in good company. The Bible records over 175 questions asked of Jesus, yet Jesus only answered a few of those questions—and in many instances, instead of an answer, he told a story. God didn't answer Job's or Moses's questions about their pain or fears either. We so desperately want life and its problems to be solved and wrapped up with a pretty, tidy bow like a Sunday sermon or a thirty-minute television drama, but that just doesn't happen. I can promise you this: You aren't alone in this journey. Jesus, referred to in Scripture as a "man of sorrows," understands pain and walks with you through this. "He was despised and rejected—a man of sorrows, acquainted with deepest grief. We turned our backs on him and looked the other way. He was despised, and we did not care" (Isa. 53:3 NLT).

143

When pain strikes our lives, we desperately desire to see God's power, yet we abhor and retreat from the experiences that best demonstrate it. God's power is best demonstrated in our painful weaknesses. There he opens our eyes to his power, might, grace, and love. Many biblical greats have endured pain worse than we could imagine. (When was the last time you imagined yourself alone in a well, thrown in prison, or surrounded by armies?) And they offer us lessons to take with us through our own journeys.

In Hebrews 12:1, we read about "the great cloud of witnesses" who have gone before us. Many of them endured great pain and offer lessons for us if we're willing to consider their plight, their journey, how they processed their pain, how God responded, and the lessons they learned.

Several of these courageous sufferers come to my mind easily: God gave Moses Aaron and Hur to help hold up his arms when he was weary in battle. *The prayers of others strengthen us for battle too.* The woman with the issue of blood merely needed to touch the hem of Jesus's garment, and he never shamed her for it. He loved her and healed her. *Today we reach for his hem.* Daniel was never alone when he remained in the lions' den. *Now we depend on God as our companion through our pain as well.* When the widow of Zarephath was obedient to God, he provided her and her son enough oil and flour to last them years during the drought and famine. *God promises to provide for our needs also.* I love David's example: He didn't worry about how big Goliath seemed because he knew how big God was. *Today, we choose to focus on the size of our God instead of the depth of our pain.*

Yet some stories made such a weighty impression on my painful journey that they deserve greater consideration.

Jabez

Consider Jabez, his life, and his influence. "Jabez was more honorable than his brothers. His mother had named him Jabez,

144

saying, 'I gave birth to him in pain.' Jabez cried out to the God of Israel, 'Oh, that you would bless me and enlarge my territory! Let your hand be with me, and keep me from harm so that I will be free from pain.' And God granted his request" (1 Chron. 4:9–10). Scripture tells us our words have the power of life or death, blessing or cursing. Can you imagine your mother giving you a name that means "birthed in pain"? What a curse. And yet Jabez refused to let his moniker define him. He prayed and declared his trust in God to free him from pain. The lesson in our painful journey? *Prayerfully trust God to heal the source of our pain.*

The Woman with the Issue of Blood

Matthew, Mark, and Luke all recount the story of the gentile woman from Caesarea who endured a disease that caused her to hemorrhage for twelve years. In her culture, women who bled were considered unclean and were ostracized. As I recall childhood bullying and ostracizing, my heart grieves for this woman and the pain she endured physically, emotionally from the shame and loneliness, relationally from her isolation, financially from her likely inability to work, and spiritually from her disqualification from participating in religious ceremonies and customs. Her physical impurity essentially excluded her from normal life and left her rejected by society and many of the individuals around her. In Mark's account, he notes that nothing improved her situation, and it only worsened over time (Mark 5:26).

The account of this woman's plight is sandwiched within the greater story of Jairus calling Jesus to help his ailing daughter. The woman's community considered her a bruised reed—broken and worthless. Yet she demonstrated great faith. Her impurity as well as the sheer mass of the crowd made it virtually impossible for her to approach Jesus, yet she displayed great resolve and determination to reach the least-noticed aspect of his attire. Her painful desperation made her willing, and she received great reward for her faith-filled efforts. Jesus stopped on the way to Jairus's home, acknowledged that power had left him, and attended to the most rejected woman in the crowd. Prior to her encounter with Jesus, she had exhausted all her resources without success, but an encounter with Jesus forever altered the trajectory of the rest of her life. We may not know the woman's name, but we know her situation and her painful need, and Jesus ensured that we would know of her faith for the rest of time.

The lesson to us in our pain? *Against all odds, despite what others say or how they believe, keep walking in faith, believing in God's power to heal, while reaching for the hem of his garment. God is a rewarder of faith.*

Paul

Paul suffered great pain throughout his ministry. He says, "I was given a thorn in my flesh, a messenger from Satan to torment me and keep me from becoming proud" (2 Cor. 12:7 NLT). We don't know if the thorn he suffered was a physical ailment, emotional torment, a spiritual attack, or even relational pain. This perhaps makes it easier to relate not only to his pain but also to his desire for God to remove it. He asked God three times to remove the thorn but didn't get the result he sought; rather God told him that his grace was sufficient in Paul's pain.

Through this painful trial, Paul gained an appreciation for his pain and resulting weakness because it highlighted God's grace and strength. Paul says, "That is why, for Christ's sake, I delight in weaknesses, in insults, in hardships, in persecutions, in difficulties. For when I am weak, then I am strong" (2 Cor. 12:10). His declaration, "I delight," indicates that he thought good of what others might only consider punishment at the hand of God. Instead of blaming, accusing, or resenting God for his pain, Paul trusted that his heavenly Father knew best, and he welcomed his grace and the clarity that came with it to understand its value in his life. Paul's revelation regarding his pain reminds us that God never withholds good from his children and that our job is to trust that ultimately God truly does work all things for our good and for his glory (see Rom. 8:28).

God never chastised Paul for his plea that God remove the thorn, yet he also didn't give Paul the response he desired. Instead of rescuing Paul, God extended grace to endure. What a gift that is! My greatest desire is that my journey through pain will offer a platform for God's power and will result in a testimony and undebatable witness to God's great mercy and grace. Our lesson? *Accept that God's answer is his best for us and trust him to work it for our good and his glory.*

Jacob

Genesis 32:22–32 recounts Jacob's experience wrestling God in human form. This occurred the night before Jacob was to reconnect with his older brother, a warlord and leader of men whom Jacob had cheated out of his birthright decades earlier. That night Jacob encountered a man and wrestled with him through the night. At dawn the man sought to separate, "but Jacob replied, 'I will not let you go unless you bless me'" (v. 26). Genesis goes on to tell us, "Then he blessed him there. So Jacob called the place Peniel, saying, 'It is because I saw God face to face, and yet my life was spared'" (vv. 29–30).

Jacob's wrestling occurred at night, a time when the distractions of the day have settled, and when we're left to face our own weaknesses and wrongdoings. Jacob's heritage came from Abraham, the father of many nations, yet his behavior was a familial disgrace. But in verses 27–28, God renames him Israel, giving him a *new* identity, highlighting that our identity comes only from Christ. Only God could truly forgive Jacob's lifelong mistreatment of his brother for his own gain. Jacob displayed tenacity in his wrestling of the mysterious man. Jacob certainly didn't deserve a blessing but persevered until he received it. Jacob's wrestling match left him lame and limping but simultaneously blessed. Perhaps his greatest blessing was a life-altering encounter *with* God after previously only knowing *about* God. Jacob's experience offers us many lessons to consider: We do not deserve God's blessings through our own merit, yet we have them through the blood of Jesus. *Perhaps we too should wrestle with God, persevering and seeking the blessing of a fresh encounter with a living God and learning our true identity in Christ.*

> **Perhaps we too should wrestle with God, persevering and seeking the blessing of a fresh encounter with a living God and learning our true identity in Christ.**

Elijah

In 1 Kings 19, we read the story of Elijah, who fled for his life into the wilderness of Judah after being threatened by Jezebel, queen to Israel's King Ahab and instigator of the murder of the prophets of God. As Elijah sat under a tree, he pleaded in despair for God to take his life. There, God miraculously provided food and water before calling Elijah to a forty-day journey. At the end of the journey, Elijah was at Mount Sinai, where God originally met his people and gave them the law through Moses. God questioned Elijah about his flight and brought Elijah to confront his own fear of being the only one left of God's called people. God directed Elijah to several actions, including anointing two kings and Elijah's own successor. Elijah went on to resume his leadership as a prophet in Israel until God chose to demonstrate his power over death by bringing Elijah to himself in the original chariot of fire.

Elijah was generally a bold man, given God's power, and yet he came to the place where his pain was too great to handle by himself. God never turned his back on Elijah or chastised him in his perceived weakness. Instead, God challenged Elijah's understanding of himself and of God. Elijah had great faith, but he still encountered painful circumstances that were too great to handle by himself, revealing his ultimate dependence on God Almighty. One of the great lessons we can glean from Elijah's painful experience is that *God answered Elijah with the gift of God himself, and he will do the same for us.*

Naomi and Ruth

The book of Ruth tells us about Naomi, a Hebrew wife and mother. A famine in her hometown of Bethlehem prompted a move to the neighboring country of Moab. Loss ushered in pain and grief when her husband and their two sons died, leaving Naomi a childless widow in a foreign country and without any means of support.

Those who have lost a spouse or children can relate to Naomi's despair—she was so devastated that she declared she no longer wanted to be referred to as Naomi, which in English means "pleasant," but instead as Mara, which means "bitter." In her culture, names were a declaration or a summary of one's experience, and Naomi's adoption of the name Mara reflects the intensity of her grief, bitterness, and the possible anger toward God that resulted from her pain.

Naomi decided to return to Bethlehem and tried to convince her two widowed daughters-in-law to remain in Moab where they had better prospects of finding new husbands. One did, but the other, Ruth, committed to staying with Naomi and caring for her. This Moabite widow, who had nothing to recommend her to the people of Mara's hometown and no means of support other than gathering the leavings from the local wheat fields, was

149

provided for by God through marriage and blessed to become the great-grandmother of King David and an ancestor of Jesus.

Naomi and Ruth grieved their losses, but God led them to a place of great provision as well as participation in the unfolding of his plan of redemption leading to the birth of our Savior and our reconciliation with God. Our lesson? *Even when our situations are painful and seem desolate, following God's leading makes room for his reconciliation, restoration, and redemption not only for ourselves but also for others.*

Mary Magdalene

Any discussion regarding pain experienced by those during biblical times ought to include a discussion regarding Mary Magdalene. She is first introduced into the narrative in Luke 8:1–3:

> After this, Jesus traveled about from one town and village to another, proclaiming the good news of the kingdom of God. The Twelve were with him, and also some women who had been cured of evil spirits and diseases: Mary (called Magdalene) from whom seven demons had come out; Joanna the wife of Chuza, the manager of Herod's household; Susanna; and many others. These women were helping to support them out of their own means.

In Mary's culture, the demon-possessed were generally the outcasts of society, considered of little worth, isolated, and demeaned. If you've ever been bullied or abused in some fashion, you know the pain that follows. If I put myself in Mary's sandals prior to her encounter with Jesus, I imagine she likely felt very alone, marginalized, and ostracized . . . mentally, emotionally, relationally, and likely spiritually pained, but quite possibly also physically pained by the possessing spirits and the "diseases" that are left vague and unnamed in Scripture.

Little is known about Mary's history, and Scripture offers scant details of the miracle of Jesus casting seven demons from her. If you've ever suffered spiritual attack, you can imagine what a life-changing encounter Mary experienced at the healing hands of Jesus at a time when women were degraded and the demon-possessed banished and shunned from the rest of society. It would have been nothing out of the ordinary for Jesus, who healed many throughout his ministry, but it was a defining moment for Mary. In a time when women were considered less significant members of society, Mary was mentioned at least twelve times in Scripture, more than many of Jesus's disciples. Relatively few individuals are named in the Bible, but those mentioned are meant to be remembered. Several times when a group of women are mentioned in the New Testament, Mary is mentioned first, a sign of her significance. Mary possessed such gratitude for Jesus's impact on her life that she financially supported Jesus's ministry, traveled with Jesus and the disciples, helped prepare his body for burial, was the last to leave the cross but the first to appear at his tomb following his resurrection, and was the first individual Jesus appeared to after she found his tomb empty.

Mary's life of pain was significant, but what she did with her life following her healing by Jesus became more significant. A lesson for us: *Just as in Mary Magdalene's story, Jesus's offer of redemption draws us to a greater focus on him and a lesser focus on our life of pain.*

Jesus

Jesus experienced pain in many forms, most notably emotional, relational, spiritual, physical, and grief. He took on human form to come to a world that rejected, betrayed, and spat on him. Mocked, tortured, condemned, beaten, and crucified, he experienced pain far greater than we will ever know so that we might experience forgiveness, redemption, and a restored relationship with our heavenly Father. When Lazarus, one of his closest friends, died, Jesus wept and was "deeply moved in

151

spirit and troubled" (John 11:33). Jesus modeled grief for us, as a gift to process our loss.

We read of Jesus's agonizing pain when he cried out to his Father to spare his life the night before his crucifixion. "In the days of his flesh, Jesus offered up prayers and supplications, with loud cries and tears, to him who was able to save him from death" (Heb. 5:7 ESV). On the cross he cried, "My God, my God, why have you forsaken me?" (Matt. 27:46), feeling rejected and abandoned by his Father.

Jesus modeled obedience to God even unto his own unjust, tormenting death, because he knew of the greater purpose in his suffering. The lesson to us? *Don't give in to the enemy's temptation to reject God in our pain, but rather trust that God did not cause our pain and that he will use it for a greater purpose than we can fathom.*

God desires not only the obedience of our hands but also the gift of our hearts given willingly in love to him. Ultimately that requires our trust despite our longing to understand why, what, and when in response to our questions regarding life's pain. That's what Job, the woman with the issue of blood, Jesus, and these others in Scripture exemplified. Perhaps as part of God's healing our pain, he desires to teach us greater lessons that could not be achieved another way. What is he teaching you through your pain?

The Hem of His Garment

Trust in the LORD with all your heart
    and lean not on your own understanding;
in all your ways submit to him,
    and he will make your paths straight.

Proverbs 3:5–6

----------------------------------- **Your Rx** -----------------------------------

1. Consider the pain accounts of those mentioned above from Scripture or of others. With whom do you most identify and why? Ask God what lesson he has for you from their experiences.

2. Prayerfully ask God to reveal what lessons he's been teaching you through your pain journey and record them to encourage yourself in the future.

3. Look up 2 Corinthians 12:10; Psalm 27:13; and Proverbs 3:5–6. Write the verses on index cards and place them where you will see them frequently. Read these passages aloud three times daily, committing them to memory. Ask God to reveal himself to you in your pain.

My Prayer for You

Father, my heartfelt cry is that you will encourage with the accounts written in your Word the heart of this dear one who is journeying through pain. You are gracious to guide us through the experiences and accounts of those who came before us, who endured, and who encountered you as a result. Thank you for the gift of faith you build in us. Strengthen this precious child of yours to trust you for the healing that you most know they need. Help them to keep walking in faith and continue reaching for your hem. Guide them to accept your answer as being best for their situation and to know that you will bring good from it. Forgive us when we resist and complain, wanting our way, but help us to experience you afresh. Through our pain bring reconciliation, restoration, and redemption, and use our pain for a greater purpose. In Jesus's name, amen.

Recommended Playlist

"I'll Find You," Lecrae, © 2017 by Reach Records, LLC

"Same God," Elevation Worship, © 2022 by Elevation
Worship Records

"Before Me," Holly Halliwell, © 2022 by Anthem Records

"Heroes," Amanda Cook, © 2015 by Bethel Music

11

Flip the Script on Pain

We stood in the kitchen chatting with our dear friend, the first friend we made after moving to Texas to start our family. She connected people like no one else I'd ever known, and if a need was known, she quickly filled it or found someone who could. We had known each other fifteen years when, on the same day my first book released, my husband was diagnosed with cancer for the second time. Our attention shifted from book-release parties and marketing to doctors' appointments, surgery, and chemotherapy. Without any hesitation, my friend recruited all her friends and set up a meal train to feed our family while we managed the medical care.

Our friendship had prevailed through her divorce, my husband's first cancer diagnosis, the death of her two sons, her cancer diagnosis and treatment, and then a second type of cancer for my husband. She knew us to our core: what we believed, how we behaved in public and behind closed doors, and the fight my husband and I possessed. While she lamented our new plight, not wishing it on anyone, she shared what seemed to me to be the most profound perspective I had heard: "What if this cancer diagnosis isn't even about y'all?" (She was from Texas after all!) "What if it is about the people who are going to be impacted by the testimony of your lives as you endure it?"

Her statement resonated with my spiritual discernment, and I knew God had prompted her to say that. It flipped the script on my pain and changed how we viewed not only that painful experience but every painful trial since then. What if our pain is part of a bigger, kingdom-focused picture?

Pain and Suffering Are Universal

We tend to view pain as a bad thing. God offers us the opportunity to flip the script on pain and learn its value in our lives. He did not create his children for pain but to walk in a relationship with him. Yet since the wayward behavior of Adam and Eve, pain has been a universal experience. The suffering of some may be more intense or require greater perseverance, but everyone will experience pain of some kind in their lives. God uses affliction, pain, and suffering in our lives to refine us and mature us to better reflect him, like a loving father does with his beloved children.

> And have you completely forgotten this word of encouragement that addresses you as a father addresses his son? It says,
>
> > "My son, do not make light of the Lord's discipline,
> > and do not lose heart when he rebukes you,
> > because the Lord disciplines the one he loves,
> > and he chastens everyone he accepts as his son."
>
> Endure hardship as discipline; God is treating you as his children. For what children are not disciplined by their father?

156

If you are not disciplined—and everyone undergoes discipline—then you are not legitimate, not true sons and daughters at all. (Heb. 12:5–8)

The writer of Hebrews in fact indicates that to *not* have afflictions or pain and suffering in our life would be to *not* have the admonition of God, which would mean we are not his child. I've had friends and acquaintances whom I've thought of as "pre-believers" because they had not yet discovered their need for a saving relationship with Jesus. And I've considered that their lives have appeared easy, without any major trials, hurts, or pain. Considering this passage in Hebrews, I would rather have my pain than their ease.

> **We tend to view pain as a bad thing. God offers us the opportunity to flip the script on pain and learn its value in our lives.**

During my most painful trials, I've grown impatient and discouraged, at times despising the pain and longing for its end. Yet, God's Word encourages us not to despise pain or become discouraged by it. This is a tall order, but God never commands anything he won't help us accomplish if we seek him. He encourages us to be patient, trusting that suffering is for our benefit and that there is "a harvest of righteousness and peace" for those who endure (Heb. 12:11).

Pain Indicates That Something Is Wrong

My first reaction to pain of any variety is displeasure and avoidance. I prefer a life without pain and suffering. Yet I've come to appreciate the gift of pain—physical, emotional, relational, or other—because it signals that something is wrong. Something is amiss in my body, in a relationship, in my walk with God, in my finances or work, or in other areas of my life. Pain is a natural reaction to injury or infection. If we never felt pain, potential danger would catch us unawares.

Despite the gift of pain to alert us to dis-ease, our memory of pain can prolong the release of stress hormones into our brain and body even when the threat of pain no longer exists. In *The Body Keeps the Score*, Bessel van der Kolk posits, "Trauma is not just an event that took place sometime in the past; it is also the imprint left by that experience on mind, brain, and body. This imprint has ongoing consequences for how the human organism manages to survive in the present."[1] He goes on to say, "The greatest sources of our suffering are the lies we tell ourselves."[2]

Pain Alerts Us to Faulty Thinking

Perhaps in addition to pain alerting us to something being wrong physically, emotionally, relationally, or spiritually, it also serves to alert us to faulty thinking. For any painful event, or for any significant event in our lives, we generate some cognitive framework for understanding and handling it, complete with an origin story, assumptions, and conclusions. Without appropriate deliberation and guidance from God's Holy Spirit, these frameworks can be drawn from faulty materials and assembled with wrong assumptions and conclusions. God calls us to flip the script and seek our understanding of this world in his Word, and to draw on his wisdom for the means to navigate it. Here is some of the clarity he offers to replace our faulty thinking:

Faulty Thought	→	God's Truth
God abandoned me in my suffering.	→	God never leaves us (see Deut. 31:6).

Faulty Thought	→	God's Truth
God is punishing me with pain.	→	God doesn't punish us with pain but does use it (see John 9:2–3).
If God loved me, he wouldn't have let this happen to me.	→	God loves with an everlasting love (see Jer. 31:3).
No good can come out of my situation.	→	What the enemy intended for harm God will use for good (see Gen. 50:20).
God ignores my prayers.	→	God actually turns his ear to hear us when we pray (see Ps. 116:2).

What others would you add to the list of lies you've accepted in your painful journey? What does God's Word say about those thoughts?

Pain Highlights Our Lack of Control

Our experience with pain teaches us just how little we control. While we may not be able to control what happens to us, we can choose how we will respond. Will we lament, or will we complain? Will we give up, or will we choose to persevere? Will we walk away, or will we choose to trust God even when we don't understand and honestly don't like our circumstances?

Frequently, in the case of physical pain, we cannot control the root of the pain: things like injury, aging, or disease. We can follow doctors' advice or prescriptions, and we can engage in health-promoting behaviors such as exercise and healthy nutrition, but even then, for many sufferers, pain remains unrestrained.

We lack any control over the cruel, rejecting, gossiping, or lying words of another about us or to us. Even when their perception is not reality and we stand before God with a clear conscience, we can't influence what some may perceive or believe about us based on the words of others. We can control our response, though, whether we take offense, retaliate, confront, or defend. We also have the choice to explain the painful situation to our heavenly Father in as much detail as we like, ask him to offload the heavy emotional and social burden, and seek from him healing for our wounded heart.

Scripture tells us that God numbers our days (see Job 14:5). We have no control over when God chooses to take a friend or loved one out of our life or out of this world. We are left with grief and have control only over where we focus that emotional energy.

We can read or study our Bible, attend church, repent, fast and pray, and cry out to God, but we have no control over when or how God will choose to respond. God often seems most silent when we most desire to hear his voice. During times of God's silence, we control only our response. Do we allow ourselves to pick up an offense and get angry with God, especially when we feel we deserve an answer, or do we choose to wait in anticipation of his voice, remember his faithfulness, and trust that he hears our cries and is working on our behalf?

Pain Reveals Our Dependence on God

Realizing how little control we possess in this life, perhaps especially when it comes to our pain experience, often produces a defining moment in coming to terms with our dependence on God. Desperation makes us willing: Willing to step outside our own need for self-control and desire for independence. Willing to set aside our pride and assume an attitude of humility. Willing to open God's Word to learn what he says about our situation or that of others and to follow it. Willing to fast and pray

160

when we otherwise may not think of it. Willing to ask others to support us in prayer when we might prefer to keep a smile on our face and our pain locked up in our heart where no one can see. When all we are left with is God, we realize we need to be willing to come to him in a way we may never have before.

Never once in Scripture does God say, "You're on your own in this one"; "Fight for yourself"; or "Let me know when you have it all figured out." Instead he says, "As I was with Moses, so I will be with you; I will never leave you nor forsake you" (Josh. 1:5); "If any of you lacks wisdom, you should ask God, who gives generously to all without finding fault, and it will be given to you" (James 1:5); and "Ask me and I will tell you remarkable secrets you do not know about things to come" (Jer. 33:3 NLT).

I applaud the woman with the issue of blood because she tried everything in her own strength to heal herself, including exhausting her physical and financial resources, and Scripture says she only worsened (see Mark 5:26). When she exhausted every other avenue of healing, she engaged her faith and reached out to the Great Physician. In her weakened, frail condition, she pushed through the crowd, determined to touch Jesus's hem. She could get no lower nor any further from making eye contact with the Master. The defining moment in this woman's life occurred when, lacking in her own strength, she reached out for Jesus's hem in faith, and his strength went out from him into her, healing her of the pain that had plagued her for over a decade. This story so beautifully exemplifies our dependence on God and yet how important our faith is as we reach out to him to do what only he can do. Perhaps instead of viewing our dependence on God in a negative light, we can see it as the avenue he uses to draw us to him.

So easy to forget yet critical to remember, God is bigger than our pain. Bigger than our hurt. Bigger than our brokenness.

Bigger than our suffering. Bigger than our doubts. Bigger than our discouragement. Bigger than our scars. And because God is involved, our story and the impact it has is bigger than our pain and bigger than what we can see now. Our story isn't over, *and it isn't limited to our pain*. That's the perspective that God brings.

Pain Refocuses Us on the Present

Much of what I've learned through my pain journey is that pain causes us to be present. Pain forces our attention to the here and now. When physical pain makes our body scream, or emotional pain sears our heart, looking back on what once was or what we wish our present reality would be does us little good. Yet what if pain is an invitation from God to be present in the here and now, not alone but *with him*? God promises to be I AM (see Exod. 3:14)—not I was, or I will be, but I AM—in the here and now. In stating he is "I AM," he reminds us that he is all-encompassing (everything we ever need him to be) and all-sufficient (he never lacks the wisdom, knowledge, or resources to meet our every need in the present).

Worry, fear, anxiety, doubt, dread, shame, and regret all cause us to project ahead to an unknown future without God as I AM, or to the past, which cannot be changed. Too often, we focus on showing up perfect as opposed to present, but that's exhausting. As unpleasant as pain is, it forces us to be present but not alone. The greatest gift God gave us for the present is Jesus, who was called Immanuel, which means "God with us" (see Isa. 7:14 and Matt. 1:23).

Loneliness looms in the valley of pain, but we are promised God's eternal presence whether we're on the mountaintops or in the valley lows.

> Where can I go from your Spirit?
> Where can I flee from your presence?
> If I go up to the heavens, you are there;
>   if I make my bed in the depths you are there. (Ps.
>   139:7–8)

Macrina Wiederkehr declares, "To stand before both the difficult and the beautiful with an open heart will take some practice."[3] While pain is difficult, it is also beautiful when we view it as an invitation to be present with the One who loves us more than life itself.

Perfected through Pain and Suffering

I frequently receive messages from other pain sufferers either offering encouragement that can only come from knowing pain themselves or seeking encouragement when pain obscures their ability to see the good in life around them. I once chatted with another pain sufferer, who lamented, "I don't want to go on anymore. I don't want to continue seeing doctors or taking medicine or attending therapy. I no longer resemble my former self at all. I don't feel like me anymore, and I don't like what I see staring back at me in the mirror." Her sentiments reflected attitudes similar to those I experienced at different points in my pain journey. I knew not to offer platitudes, clichés, or spiritual Band-Aids guised in Bible verses. Rather I offered a listening ear and an empathic heart. I tendered my presence so she knew she didn't journey alone. Because I have suffered, I can empathize. In the same way, we all have One who can empathize with our pain and suffering.

Scripture reveals that Jesus was made perfect through suffering. "In bringing many sons and daughters to glory, it was fitting that God, for whom and through whom everything exists, should make the pioneer of their salvation perfect through what he suffered" (Heb. 2:10). Even in the life of God's own Son suffering was necessary to perfect him. Additionally, his suffering made him merciful and faithful to us, his children.

> For this reason he had to be made like them, fully human in every way, in order that he might become a merciful and faithful high priest in service to God, and that he might make atonement for the sins of the people. Because he himself suffered when he was tempted, he is able to help those who are being tempted. (Heb. 2:17–18)

Pain offers us the opportunity to have the rough and unholy edges rubbed off us, and it teaches us how to extend mercy and grace to others. Frequently God allows pain and suffering to spur us on to growth in who we are, whose we are, and who he is for us. The more painful the battle, the greater the opportunity for growth and the greater our appreciation for his work in us.

God uses pain and suffering to teach us, refine us, and renew our faith. "Therefore we do not lose heart. Though outwardly we are wasting away, yet inwardly we are being renewed day by day. For our light and momentary troubles are achieving for us an eternal glory that far outweighs them all. So we fix our eyes not on what is seen, but on what is unseen, since what is seen is temporary, but what is unseen is eternal" (2 Cor. 4:16–18). To follow Christ is to accept the suffering that comes with the journey. "But rejoice inasmuch as you participate in the sufferings of Christ, so that you may be overjoyed when his glory is revealed" (1 Pet. 4:13). After we

> The more painful the battle, the greater the opportunity for growth and the greater our appreciation for his work in us.

endure pain, our perception of the world is divided into those who know or understand and those who don't. In this lifetime, we may never realize the role we play in other people's lives, but one day in glory we will see that impact, including the value of the compassion and sensitivity developed from our pain. May our pain make us more sensitive to the pain and suffering of others and help us to be a conduit of God's compassion, comfort, and love.

The Hem of His Garment

And the God of all grace, who called you to his eternal glory in Christ, after you have suffered a little while, will himself restore you and make you strong, firm and steadfast.

1 Peter 5:10

Your Rx

1. God's kingdom often operates from an upside-down perspective relative to the world. How has your pain journey taught you to view things more from God's perspective than from your own or the world's?

2. Prayerfully ask God to reveal any faulty thinking or lies you've believed that don't align with the truth from his Word. Record them, then find and record truths from God's Word that refute them so you can refer back to his truths when the lies resurface.

3. Look up Hebrews 12:9–11; Genesis 50:20; and 2 Corinthians 4:16–18. Write the verses on index cards and place them where you will see them frequently. Read these passages aloud three times daily, committing them to memory. Ask God to reveal himself to you in your pain.

My Prayer for You

Father, it is my prayer that your Holy Spirit will give this dear one a fresh revelation and help them hear your voice as you walk with them through their pain. We humbly come before you, offering gratitude and thanksgiving that you take what the enemy intended for evil in our lives and use it for good. Thank you that we no longer need to feel singled out or punished because we endure pain, since pain is a universal experience. Help this fellow pain sufferer to flip the script on pain and see their pain through your perspective. Thank you that when we allow it to, pain can be a great teacher. Thank you for teaching us through pain just how dependent we are on you, how little control we have, the importance of focusing on the present, and how you used pain to perfect even Jesus. Give us your perspective on pain. In Jesus's name, amen.

Recommended Playlist

"Look What You've Done," Tasha Layton, © 2021 by BEC Recordings

"More Than Ever," After Grace, © 2022 by GraceTalk Studio

"Desert Road," Casting Crowns, © 2022 by Provident Label Group, LLC

"Show Me Where You Were," Laney Rene, © 2022 by Laney Rene Music

12

Dos and Don'ts

In my pain journey over the past decade, I've made a book full of mistakes and learned some hard-fought lessons. Looking back, I can see where my thoughts went off the track and into a dead end. There were times when I retreated from battle, times when I misappropriated blame, and times when I was blind to the truth. Life is a valuable teacher because after doing things suboptimally, I'm likely to course-correct more quickly now. My prior MO tragically included jumping in and working harder to compensate for the losses I felt. I also tended to overreact in misdirected anger, which I now realize was driven by great fear, frustration, and dread. After enduring significant relational and secondary pain, I learned to be more deliberate in relationships, to share fewer details and with a smaller number of trusted confidants. I realize now that God values my prayers as much as anyone else's. He withheld answers from some of his greatest saints, and I'm willing to accept that his not answering my questions doesn't signify a lack of love or compassion on his part. I've learned to trust him more quickly and completely in my pain.

What Not to Do When You're in Pain

While some coping mechanisms help improve our mindset or outlook even if they don't eradicate our pain, in treating patients as well as walking through my own pain, I've identified some coping mechanisms we use that unintentionally exacerbate pain and should be avoided.

Don't Make Big Decisions

Pain makes everything seem like an emergency. It prompts the fight-or-flight response in our body and causes us to act quickly but often irrationally. Whenever possible, I encourage you to avoid making big decisions in the heat of pain. Consider the possibilities, write down your thoughts regarding the advantages and disadvantages of decision alternatives, and pray for wisdom. But take time so your decisions made in pain don't result in fodder for regret.

Don't Live in Regret or Fear

We have a great propensity to look at life through the rearview mirror, either in regret or in pining for our old normal. Regret chains our heart and mind to a place we have no control over. Regret keeps us bound to guilt, shame, and condemnation, none of which come from the Lord. "Therefore, there is now no condemnation for those who are in Christ Jesus" (Rom. 8:1). Looking to the past to explain away our pain and suffering leads to regret. On the contrary, looking to the future through the lens of pain promotes worry, fear, anxiety, and dread. When we're tempted to look through the rearview mirror and live in regret or to look to the future through a telescope of fear, take that as a signal to instead look up to the God who sees, knows, and promises to go before us, walk beside us, and hem us in before and behind (see Lev. 26:12; Deut. 31:8; and Ps. 139:5).

Don't Isolate

"The LORD God said, 'It is not good for the man to be alone'" (Gen. 2:18). Satan knows Scripture better than we do—he wielded it as a weapon against Christ. But Satan uses guilt, shame, and blame to push us into hiding, desiring that we believe no one else understands our pain or painful circumstances. Isolation ensures that we will not be strengthened by the common bond formed through sharing our pain. Earlier we discussed the importance of encouraging one another, but isolation hinders encouragement. We are commanded, "And let us not neglect our meeting together, as some people do, but encourage one another, especially now that the day of his return is drawing near" (Heb. 10:25 NLT). Paul suffered loneliness in prison and wrote to Timothy asking him to come visit him quickly (see 2 Tim. 4:9). In his moments of greatest pain and despair, Jesus brought Peter, James, and John with him to the garden where he prayed (see Matt. 26:36–44). It's impossible to run away from God, so let's not waste time even trying (see Ps. 139:7–13). When it comes to socializing in pain, however, not all people are created equally.

Don't Socialize with Negative People

Scripture tells us, "Above all else, guard your heart, for everything you do flows from it" (Prov. 4:23). Negativity breeds negativity. When we already struggle to keep an optimistic mindset, negative attitudes, beliefs, behaviors, and words from others just add water to an already sinking boat. It's our choice to plug the leak by intentionally (there's that word again!) choosing time with friends who, by maturity or temperament, have a positive influence and minimizing the input from those we know have a propensity for negativity. Surround yourself with those who will help you bail the water or who will throw you a life preserver when you're going under!

Don't Overshare Details

After my husband received his first cancer diagnosis, we would hear stories about people's aunt's best friend's boyfriend who died of cancer. People also offered every magic potion, elixir, and supplement they *just knew* would cure whatever ailed my husband, as well as their opinions regarding how we caused his diagnosis. I know people mean well, but even the best-intentioned people contribute to guilt, shame, and secondary pain by assuming they know what that person is going through or that they have the answer the sufferer or their doctors never thought of. In our journey, we learned to keep details to a minimum and in doing so endured less condemnation and criticism. God doesn't require others to know our pain specifics before he will answer their prayers, walk with us, comfort us, or heal us.

> Surround yourself with those who will help you bail the water or who will throw you a life preserver when you're going under!

Don't Overextend Yourself

When pain steals the best of your energy, time, outlook, and motivation, perhaps one of the most consistent and best pieces of advice I can offer and have practiced is this: simplify. Whether your pain is physical, emotional, spiritual, grief, or another type, normal, everyday tasks can require extraordinary strength, effort, or fortitude. Now is the time to simplify. Recognize and pursue the minimum that needs attention to keep life moving forward rather than extending yourself by adding new responsibilities to a plate already crowded with pain. That doesn't mean you won't be able to do more at another time, but it means you will give priority to what I call the "nonnegotiables" of life. These nonnegotiables are the things that you're not willing *not* to do, the essentials in life. In contrast to the nonnegotiables are the discretionary or extraneous tasks that you know will heighten your pain or require energy that is better applied elsewhere.

Don't Believe Lies

Letting our thought life go unchecked is a slippery slope into anxiety, depression, or despair. It takes only a fraction of a second for the enemy to lie to us and for an unguarded mind to accept the deception and incorporate it into our thinking. We must compare these lies to what we know is God's truth.

- **You're not deserving of healing.** In one sense, that's true. None of us deserve healing, mercy, grace, salvation, or any of the other gifts God extends to us. But whether we deserve them or not, Christ has already offered them and paid the price. "But he was pierced for our transgressions, he was crushed for our iniquities; the punishment that brought us peace was on him, and by his wounds we are healed" (Isa. 53:5). Jesus sees us as deserving, and he has already done the work to make our healing possible. It will happen.

- **You're a victim.** The victim mentality is the most defeating mindset we can take on. In "victimality," we become passive and surrender an active role in preparing for and pursuing healing. In doing nothing, we assume the victim identity. It is insidious because it's the easy and default mode, and our flesh, our culture, and our spiritual enemy point us here. It takes effort to avoid it. First Corinthians 15:57 assures us that we've been given victory through Jesus. And Romans 8:37 reminds us that "in all these things we are more than conquerors through him who loved us."

171

- **Your best days are behind you.** Pain causes us to look at our prior level of functioning and compare that to our current limitations. Anyone who compares their success or productivity to a previous version of themselves will have a highly skewed perspective. We as humans can't see ourselves in an honest light, and looking through the lens of pain just makes it worse. Accept instead the view that God takes of you. Jeremiah 29:11 reminds us that God's plans for us are good and include both a future and a hope. If you woke up today, God still has a purpose for your life, even if it may look different from what you thought it would.

- **You'll always hurt.** I can't promise if or when God will remove your pain this side of heaven, although I know he hurts when we hurt. But one day, we will live pain-free, and I'm looking forward to that day. "He will wipe every tear from their eyes. There will be no more death or mourning or crying or pain, for the old order of things has passed away" (Rev. 21:4). Until that day comes, remember God is a God of healing. He can't not heal. Your healing has started. It will be complete and comprehensive, even if it only feels like a crumb right now.

- **Your pain is your identity.** That's what our enemy would like you to believe because if you believe the truth about your identity, you will oppose the chaos and pain of his spiritual kingdom of darkness. Your identity is not rooted in what titles you hold, what you do, or what pain you carry but in being a child of the Most High God. Your identity is rooted in your relationship to your heavenly Father. "I will be a Father to you, and

172

you will be my sons and daughters, says the Lord Almighty" (2 Cor. 6:18).

• **Your pain makes you ineffective for God's kingdom.** The true question is, who determines our effectiveness for the kingdom of God? I've wrestled with this question repeatedly throughout my journey. But the truth is that our contribution will continue until Christ returns if we are obedient to what God asks of us. "Being confident of this, that he who began a good work in you will carry it on to completion until the day of Christ Jesus" (Phil. 1:6). It is God who does this work. Further, it is God who has prepared the "good works" for us to pursue: "For we are God's handiwork, created in Christ Jesus to do good works, which God prepared in advance for us to do" (Eph. 2:10). Your effectiveness does not stem from your job, your current project or task, your plans, or your financial status. It comes from humbly relating to your heavenly Father and following his leading in that relationship.

Don't Give Up

Earlier we discussed the idea of going *through* pain and not camping there. It's a process not a destination. Whenever I'm tempted to give up, I think of Jesus. We know that he asked God to take the cup of death from him but then resolved to honor his Father's will above his own, which involved the most egregious suffering I can imagine. If Jesus didn't give up and we are joint heirs with him (see Rom. 8:17), it's not in our DNA to give up either. Rest, possibly, but not give up. God's commands are for the present but are also forward-looking. "I will instruct you and teach you in the way you should go; I will counsel you with my loving eye on you" (Ps. 32:8).

What to Do When You're in Pain

What do you do when the pain is debilitating and you've cried so many tears, your well is dry? When the deafening lies of the enemy suggest life will always be this way? When pain has stolen the best parts of you and your body feels like it won't do what God has called you to do? When you know you should praise and worship but you don't want to? When you know what Scripture says but it doesn't comfort you? Let's talk about things we *can* do when we're in pain.

Take Things One Moment at a Time

Pain tempts us to overthink and worry about the future, which the Bible warns against several times. When we look to God for divine guidance, he usually gives only one step at a time. We tend to make big, intricate plans, but God guides us each step of the way when we look to him for wisdom and direction. "The LORD directs the steps of the godly. He delights in every detail of their lives" (Ps. 37:23 NLT).

Remember You Aren't Alone

Pain isolates and breeds loneliness. The temptation is strong to believe we're alone in our suffering and that no one understands. But the truth is that Jesus understands. "For we do not have a high priest who is unable to empathize with our weaknesses" (Heb. 4:15). Jesus loves us just as much in our pain as he does when we are healed and whole, but we may appreciate him more for his suffering on our behalf after we too have suffered. When loneliness swallows you and your hope, remember that Jesus is praying for you! "Therefore he is able to save completely those who come to God through him, because he always lives to intercede for them" (Heb. 7:25).

Engage Prayerful Support

We've discussed the importance of prayer, especially lament, while we're waiting for God to answer. But what about those times when pain is so severe that all we have are tears or groans to offer? Times when we don't know what to pray? Scripture tells us the Holy Spirit interprets our groans and prays for us through groans too deep for words (see Rom. 8:26). When you're too weak or in too much pain to pray for yourself, engage the prayerful support of family, friends, or ministry staff to lift you up. Even Moses needed Aaron and Hur to hold up his arms, so there is no shame in asking others to pray for us (see 2 Thess. 3:1).

Forgive Yourself and Others

Our need for understanding tempts us to cast blame, while our fear of being permanently rendered shattered and our desire to never be caught off guard again lead us to erect a wall of bitterness and resentment around our painful circumstance. Bitterness, resentment, and unforgiveness weaken our ability to seek and prepare for healing and only hurt us. One of the best things we can do to aid our own healing and wellness is to forgive ourselves and others. We exhibit strength when we forgive others who express no remorse or apology. It liberates us from further psychological pain and from the accrued bitterness that builds when we continue to brood over a perceived offense. Perhaps, however, the hardest person to forgive is ourselves for anything we've done to contribute to our pain or for what we didn't do to prevent it. Harboring guilt and shame just exacerbates our pain. God forgives us for everything we've ever done because of the penalty Jesus paid for us on the cross. If we don't extend forgiveness to ourselves, we might as well say, "Your sacrifice wasn't great enough for me, Jesus."

Extend Grace to Yourself and Others

Recently a friend texted to ask how a particular project was coming along. I shared my frustration at the negative impact my pain had on my productivity. She gently responded, "First take a deep breath, and slowly exhale. Now extend yourself grace for doing the best you can do given your circumstances. You've continued to press through and refused to give up." I smiled as I read her response because it sounded like something I would say to my patients or friends. Guilt and regret keep pain smoldering, but when we extend ourselves grace, we extinguish the guilt and regret. A simple way I extend grace to myself on severe pain days is by reducing the investment of my time and effort in routine activities, such as styling my hair, applying makeup, or picking the perfect outfit. Sometimes extending grace means not just taking one day at a time but taking one hour or one moment at a time and celebrating that you kept fighting.

> Guilt and regret keep pain smoldering, but when we extend ourselves grace, we extinguish the guilt and regret.

Routinely Read and Meditate on God's Word

Hebrews 4:12 says, "For the word of God is alive and active. Sharper than any double-edged sword, it penetrates even to dividing soul and spirit, joints and marrow; it judges the thoughts and attitudes of the heart." When we're fighting the pain battle, it's imperative that we use the weapons God provides us. The pain path is difficult to navigate, like driving on curvy mountain roads in the fog. But God's Word promises to guide us as a lamp and a light (see Ps. 119:105). Scripture offers perspectives that go infinitely beyond the "down in the hole" view that pain gives us. In Scripture we hear the stories of others who've walked this path before us, and we find the greatest compassion and grace from God himself toward each of us, his beloved suffering children. In routinely and regularly allowing Scripture to run through our minds by reading, memorizing, meditating, singing, or seeing a sticky note on our mirror, we develop the mental pathways that train our mind and our heart to see ourselves and our world as God does and to find a true, defensible, and available response to our pain.

Rest

When the enemy can't discourage us, he will distract us. In my most painful seasons, I've followed the tempting trail to jump in and do more to the point of burning out emotionally and physically. Physical, emotional, and spiritual exhaustion are an open door to the lazy acceptance of the enemy's lies. Just as our physical bodies require rest to rejuvenate and heal themselves, our emotions and our spirit also require rest.

Get Out of Your Own Head

In the valley of pain, I often get stuck in a cyclone of negativity, blame, resentment, and pining for a pain-free future. When that happens, I struggle to find any objectivity and instead swim in a pool of unprofitable self-pity. My tongue slices a wide berth around me and alienates those who might otherwise offer support. When I notice this—and I don't always—it's a signal to get into a different place emotionally, spiritually, mentally, or physically. This can take the form of calling a friend, fixing a cup of soup, donning my walking shoes and earbuds and hitting the street, or just turning up my praise and worship music. It may or may not include a grump session with God, but it almost always improves my serotonin levels. Severe pain calls for severe measures.

Invest in Positive Relationships

We've already discussed the dangers of social isolation and of finding affinity with negative people. The opposite of this is intuitive: to invest in positive relationships. *Intuitive* does not mean *easy*, however. Finding and maintaining good, positive friendships can be difficult in the best of times, and pain makes it that much harder. During times of pain, socializing requires intentionality or it won't happen. Set a goal to regularly seek or connect with supportive friends, both to share your heart and as an exercise to put aside your own pain and hear their heart.

Seek Others to Serve

I heard about an exchange Karl Menninger, a famous psychiatrist, had with an attendee years ago at a conference at which he was speaking, when the attendee asked something along the lines of, "If someone were thinking of ending their life, what would you tell them?" Instead of suggesting therapy or medication, Menninger essentially responded that the individual should go out the back door, walk across the railroad tracks, find someone in need, and do something to help them. He knew that altruistic behavior not only blesses the other individual but also improves our mood and takes our attention off our own situation.

Engage in Self-Care

Jesus voiced the second great commandment: that we must love others as we love ourselves (see Matt. 22:39). Too often we focus on the first aspect of his command, to love others, but the second half of that command is required first: that we love ourselves. Especially when we're in pain, self-care is critical to rebuilding our strength, emboldening our faith, and adopting a correct perspective. In caring for ourselves, we will better love and care for others.

Share Authentically

As we wait on God's deliverance from our current painful situation and as we work to live past the blot of pain that obscures the rest of life, we have an opportunity to influence the lives of others. We've seen that pain causes us to isolate, and we also know that some overdramatize their situation for the sake of gaining the attention of others. In between these poles is a space for authentically and appropriately presenting it to others, neither diminishing or hiding our pain nor spotlighting it. Doing this is complicated because we need to decide, sometimes on the spot, how much to share, when to share, and how to share. We also need to get past the fear of sharing and potentially receiving responses we've experienced before.

As believers in the redemption and continued healing work of Jesus Christ, we know we have God's own Spirit within us, a Spirit that gives us courage and that gives us wisdom, sometimes hard-won and sometimes in the moment, to discern the things we need to share authentically. Offering the encouragement we've found along the pain journey helps us link arms with others to form the common bond we've talked about.

--- **The Hem of His Garment** ---

Your righteousness, O God, reaches to the highest
     heavens.
  You have done such wonderful things.
  Who can compare with you, O God?
You have allowed me to suffer much hardship,
     but you will restore me to life again
     and lift me up from the depths of the earth.
You will restore me to even greater honor
     and comfort me once again.

                                        Psalm 71:19–21 NLT

---------------------------------- **Your Rx** ----------------------------------

1. Prayerfully consider the list of suggestions of what not to do when you're in pain to assess which of those things you need to let go of. What will you substitute them with?

2. Look over the list of common lies believed by pain sufferers. Which do you identify with? Prayerfully confess those and ask God to help you replace them with his truth.

3. Prayerfully consider the suggestions of what to do when you're in pain. Pick one or two of the suggestions to try this week. What will that activity look like for you?

4. Look up Proverbs 4:23; Isaiah 53:5; and Philippians 1:6. Write the verses on index cards and place them where you will see them frequently. Read these passages aloud three times daily, committing them to memory. Ask God to reveal himself to you in your pain.

My Prayer for You

Father, I pray for the heart of this dear one whom the enemy seeks to attack. Make them impervious to his lies. Give them strength and determination to continue believing truth. You have already taught us and provided us with everything we need for life and godliness. Pain clouds our objectivity and our ability to reason appropriate thoughts, attitudes, and behaviors. Help this dear one to seek your will, your way, and your response to know what they should and should not do in their pain. Guide their steps and help them to hear your voice above all others. In Jesus's name, amen.

Recommended Playlist

"Praise Before My Breakthrough," Bryan and Katie Torwalt, © 2018 by Sparrow Records

"There Will Be a Day," Jeremy Camp, © 2008 by Capitol CMG, Inc.

"Free," K-Anthony, © 2021 by K-Anthony

"Believe for It," CeCe Winans, © 2021 by Pure Springs Gospel, Inc.

13

Beauty for Ashes

During those days when I was on medically prescribed bed rest, tethered to an IV, in pain, and fighting to hold on to some semblance of my life, the enemy continually threw darts at my resolve. But in God's sovereignty, not immediately but over time, he turned my situation around in a way only he could. During my convalescence, all I could do was sleep, pray, listen to praise and worship music, and watch sermons online. It became my own personal retreat with God. So much so that when the doctor released me to begin to return to work, I didn't want to go. I wanted to continue cocooning with God and growing in my walk with him.

On the first day back to seeing patients at the practice, I temporarily unhooked my IV and rolled my sleeves down to cover my bruised arms. I cried from the moment I left home until a moment before my first patient walked into my office. That patient sobbed as she relayed that she didn't want to continue living. She'd had multiple surgeries, was completely bruised from all her IV treatments, and was convinced that no one understood. I wrestled with God in my mind: I don't want to tell her . . . that wouldn't be professional. *God quickly replied,* I said, tell her. *I quipped back to him,* I don't want to. I prefer to keep my pain and struggles private. *Finally, God's last retort got my attention:* You can either tell her and let me use you, or I'll find someone else who's willing to be used by me. *That settled it.*

As I handed her a tissue, she lifted her glistening eyes, barely meeting mine, before looking back at her shaking hands in her lap. I remained quiet as I unbuttoned the cuff on my sleeve and rolled it up. I knew the movement caught her attention because her eyes doubled in size as she glanced at my arm, up at my eyes, and back at my black-and-blue, swollen arm before settling on my gaze with a quizzical look. "Our situations aren't identical, but our bruises share a common story. More than anything, I want you to know you aren't alone in your pain. God sent me here today to be here for and with you."

I never wanted to go through such devastating pain and suffering. But I wanted my pain to count. And God showed me that day that my pain and suffering were not in vain. That day, and on many since then, God gave me the blessing of beauty for my ashes.

Pain Creates a Common Bond

One of our greatest desires in life is to be seen, understood, and accepted. Pain creates a common bond between sufferers and affirms that we are not alone in our suffering. "A friend loves at all times, and a brother is born for a time of adversity" (Prov. 17:17). The year of the Oklahoma City bombing was the year I interned at the University of Oklahoma Health Sciences Center in Oklahoma City. Along with my fellow interns,

184

I served with the Red Cross disaster-response team. We saw the trauma and grief of the survivors and families and of the general population. We experienced a high degree of trauma and grief ourselves simply due to our rescue involvement. Nobody in our class wanted the suffering that came with that work, but the shared experience brought a common bond, which made the tragedy more bearable. Common experiences bring us to the revelation that we are not alone in our suffering. They strengthen our resolve to persevere. At a time when some feel most alone and unseen, God brings others to come alongside us in our journey and remind us that we are seen by him. Romans 12:15 admonishes, "Rejoice with those who rejoice; mourn with those who mourn." We gain strength when we walk with others who understand and who remind us of God's truth in love.

Pain Increases Our Sensitivity and Compassion for Others

Pain and suffering teach us about the Lord's compassion for his children.

> "Though the mountains be shaken
>   and the hills be removed,
> yet my unfailing love for you will not be shaken
>   nor my covenant of peace be removed,"
>   says the LORD, who has compassion on you. (Isa.
>   54:10)

Because we are created in his image, as we experience his compassion, we grow in our sensitivity and compassion for others.

When our lives are going well and suffering is at a minimum, it's easy to slip into complacency and grow indifferent to the suffering of others. Walking through our own pain increases our sensitivity and compassion for others in a way that no other experience does. *Compassion* literally means, "suffering with another."[1] Jesus provided our best example of offering true compassion for those who grieved, for those he healed, and for humanity when he suffered and died on our behalf. Compassion is a true mark of the maturity of Christian faith. And pain reminds us of the suffering and needs of others.

In my example in the opening of this chapter, my patient knew that our common bond afforded me the chance to offer a level of understanding and compassion that others could not offer because they had not experienced the pain and suffering she had. Because of our common bond, she resolved not to give up because, to a certain degree, she would be giving up on me as well. When we see others suffering and we share about our common experience, we share the love of Christ that writes indelibly on their heart, "And over all these virtues put on love, which binds them all together in perfect unity" (Col. 3:14).

Pain and Suffering Strengthen Our Faith

Our faith in God sustains us through our suffering, and in holding fast to our faith, we see it grow through the painful trials. "For every child of God defeats this evil world, and we achieve this victory through our faith" (1 John 5:4 NLT).

I don't know what pain you're suffering or what stresses are in your life, but let me encourage you to hold on. When pain afflicts our lives, we must guard against the negative, questioning thoughts we have about God. God's Word tells us to wait on the Lord. It also tells us to be of good courage (see Ps. 27:14). Some days we need to muster courage just to get out of bed and face the day. Courage is not the absence of fear, pain, doubt, or discouragement, but rather it is the determination to push through despite them. But when we wait on God *and* maintain our courage, Scripture says that he will strengthen our hearts (see Ps. 31:24 KJV). He will bring us through stronger than we started. Better! What a blessing for focusing on God through our pain and suffering.

Pain Teaches Us Perseverance

Pain tempts us to give up, in life and on God. And doing so would steal the hope of those who are watching from the sidelines and borrowing the hope we exercise in Christ. Scripture reminds us that those who persevere receive God's blessings of both compassion and mercy because perseverance comes at a cost. "As you know, we count as blessed those who have persevered. You have heard of Job's perseverance and have seen what the Lord finally brought about. The Lord is full of compassion and mercy" (James 5:11).

Jesus modeled perseverance throughout his ministry and as he endured the greatest pain imaginable as an example for us to hold on to when we are tempted to give up. I've often said, and I fully believe, Jesus never gave up, so it's not in my DNA.

> **Jesus never gave up, so it's not in my DNA.**

When life is easy, perseverance isn't required. But pain and suffering test our ability to endure and persevere because our first instinct is to give up. Jesus persevered through pain to encourage us not to grow weary or lose heart so that in our own pain, we would continue to persevere.

Therefore, since we are surrounded by such a great cloud of witnesses, let us throw off everything that hinders and the sin that so easily entangles. And let us run with perseverance the race marked out for us, fixing our eyes on Jesus, the pioneer and perfecter of faith. For the joy set before him he endured the cross, scorning its shame, and sat down at the right hand of the throne of God. Consider him who endured such opposition from sinners, so that you will not grow weary and lose heart. (Heb. 12:1–3)

Pain Produces a Deeper Appreciation of God's Character

Pain casts doubt in our minds regarding God's character and the truth of his Word. In our pain we are tempted to blame God and think that he is somehow against us. This is common, but it is reactionary; it stems from the hurt and our instinctive response. Even Adam and Eve hid out of fear of God's anger with them. With some reflection it is possible to see that, despite the presence and intensity of pain, there is much more in our lives that is not painful than is painful. It's just that the painful part wants to have center stage and push out the rest. In learning to look past the painful part of life, we can see—even if just in glimpses—the continuing goodness of God in our lives. In this we gain a deeper appreciation of God's character, especially his love, his goodness, and his faithfulness. Pain reveals God's desire to uphold us. "The LORD upholds all who fall and lifts up all who are bowed down" (Ps. 145:14).

God knows the end from the beginning. We see only one piece of the puzzle, while he sees the entire masterpiece. Trust him. Wait on him with courage. Don't be in such a hurry to complete the puzzle and rush through the painful trials that you miss the reward at the end. He will leave you stronger and better than you began.

> Wait on the LORD;
>   Be of good courage,
>   And He shall strengthen your heart. (Ps. 27:14
>   NKJV)

Pain Grows Our Trust in God

When we have nothing left but ourselves, God, and our pain, we realize God is enough. Job lost everything of importance to him. His friends and wife attempted to convince him to curse God for not protecting him, healing him, or rescuing him. He stayed faithful to what he knew to be true about God, even as he questioned God's purpose for his suffering. Despite his friends' and wife's harsh criticism and poor advice, Job held fast to his trust in God. Through Job's faithfulness and his desire to hold fast to God, he experienced God in a new and fresh way that could only have been achieved through suffering and his clinging to the hem of God's garment: "My ears had heard of you but now my eyes have seen you" (Job 42:5). In the most painful days, our trust in God will be most tested. As we stretch our trust muscle, God reveals more of himself.

Fruit Grows in the Valleys

Patients come into my office because they hurt and their life circumstances are painfully difficult to bear. I talk with many people, both inside and outside my office, who are struggling and going through difficult times and are in pain's valley. Often, they wonder why. I have found, both personally and professionally, that so often, knowing the answer to why doesn't really help that much. It doesn't help when people get the answer to why a spouse had an affair or why a child attempted suicide or why a coworker abuses substances. The why usually doesn't make us feel better. Job asked God why, and God never answered that question.

So often, people want to live on the mountaintop. Don't we all love the mountaintop experiences? They are fulfilling and exciting and joyful. Mountaintops are wonderful for the view and the inspiration. But fruit doesn't grow on the mountaintops; it grows in the valleys.

If you are going through a painful valley journey right now, I encourage you that God never wastes our pain. Scripture says that what the enemy intended for harm, God will use for good (see Gen. 50:20). When we are in the valley, there is no place to look but up. Sometimes that is when we can most clearly see what God is doing. Sometimes in the valley, we can't see what he is doing, but we can most clearly see our need for him. Even if you can't see what God is doing, know that, just like fruit, God is growing you, maturing you, and strengthening you in that valley. So, if you are in the valley right now, let me encourage you that it serves a purpose. Mountaintops are great, but the valley is where fruit grows.

When God Uses Our Pain for Good

You never know when God might use you unexpectedly. But if there's one thing I know, it is that *God uses pain for good.* "And we know that God causes everything to work together for the good of those who love God and are called according to his purpose for them" (Rom. 8:28 NLT).

On a Sunday some time ago, our worship service ended as it always does, with our pastor inviting anyone in need of prayer to come to the front of the sanctuary to pray with one of the lay volunteers. These volunteers are available to listen to congregants' burdens and to pray with them. I had long felt a tug at my spirit to offer my time in that capacity, but I hadn't pursued it. I had always listened to others' prayers and never felt mine were as eloquent or as poised or powerful.

> If there's one thing I know, it is that *God uses pain for good.*

Yet on this Sunday, the need was great. Every volunteer was busy praying, and other congregants waited in line to receive prayer. The volunteer coordinator came over and asked if I would step in to help, so I agreed to.

No sooner had I advanced to the front of the church than a sweet lady approached me in tears. She shared that she battled depression and struggled to trust God. I smiled as I looked into her eyes and responded, "He sees you. He loves you. It's no accident that you are standing before me today. I've been where you are, and he brought me out on the other side." Her eyes, while still glistening from tears, brightened because she knew I understood her pain. She knew she could trust me with her hurts as we cried together and brought her brokenness and desperation to God in prayer.

Shared Experiences

When I was crawling in the valley of depression, you would have been hard-pressed to convince me that anything good would have come from that experience. But that time made me press in deeper to my relationship with God. It showed me there was purpose in pain. It also prompted a deeper level of understanding and compassion for others who walk through that dark valley and feel alone.

Through it, God taught me the importance of addressing the spiritual aspects of depression to find true help, hope, and healing. Now that he has brought me out the other side, he often gives me the opportunity to offer the same comfort to others. "Praise be to the God and Father of our Lord Jesus Christ, the Father of compassion and the God of all comfort, who comforts us in all our troubles, so that we can comfort those in any trouble with the comfort we ourselves receive from God" (2 Cor. 1:3–4).

Often, we cannot relate to experiences unless we have been through them personally. Depression is one of them. Now that I've walked that dark and lonely valley, I have much greater understanding and compassion for others who presently walk that road. My heart goes out to them from a place of knowing. While the specifics of our experiences may be different, I can relate on a level of shared pain, and I can enter in with them from a perspective of "Me too!" that I never could have if I had not traveled that road myself.

Walking with another in their pain is a beautiful thing, and it brings beauty for our own ashes—a blessing that a pain-free life cannot afford. My journey through the pain of physical deformity, depression and anxiety, miscarriage, rejection and betrayal, cancer, caregiving, and empty nesting allows me to enter in with others who suffer, which blesses them and me. Jesus's own experience of suffering and pain allows him to sympathize with our suffering. In your pain today, let me encourage you that God sees. He is with you, and he will use your pain for your good and for his glory in his perfect way and perfect time. God never calls the equipped—he equips those he calls. Our experiences qualify us for his service. God uses our pain for good. Our pain is never wasted. Look back on your pain journey—where can God uniquely use you to enter in with another?

The Hem of His Garment

Those who sow with tears
will reap with songs of joy.
Psalm 126:5

Your Rx

1. Consider how you've experienced a common bond with others because of your pain journey.
2. Reflect on the different blessings from suffering mentioned above. Which have you noticed in your own pain journey? How so?

3. Look up Isaiah 54:10; 1 John 5:4; and Hebrews 12:1–3. Write the verses on index cards and place them where you will see them frequently. Read these passages aloud three times daily, committing them to memory. Ask God to reveal himself to you in your pain.

My Prayer for You

Father, you know the hurts and the cries of the one reading this page right now. You see the tears and you know the pain. Your Word tells us that you are near to the brokenhearted and you save those who are crushed in spirit. I ask now, Lord, that you would be especially close to your child who is hurting. That you would extend comfort and lend shelter under your wing. That you would renew their strength. And that by your sovereign hand, you would bring good from whatever the enemy intended for evil, and that you would bring beauty for the painful ashes they are enduring. Comfort even now so that one day they may comfort others with the same comfort you offer today. In Jesus's precious name I pray, amen.

Recommended Playlist

"No Hopeless Soul," Stephen Stanley, © 2021 by Capitol CMG, Inc.

"Peace," Anna Golden, © 2020 by Capitol CMG, Inc.

"Do It for Me," Grace Graber, © 2022 by Grace Graber

"Whatever It Costs," Rachel Morley, © 2020 by Zeo Music Worship

In Celebration of YOU!

Dear Survivor,

I'm so proud of you, and I hope you are as well. You didn't give in when pain threatened to pull you under. You didn't give up when the enemy demanded you quit. Instead, you did the most challenging thing and persevered through the most painful days, and you have a testimony to share for it.

Habakkuk 3:19 declares, "The Lord God is my Strength, my personal bravery, and my invincible army; He makes my feet like hinds' feet and will make me to walk [not to stand still in terror, but to walk] and make [spiritual] progress upon my high places [of trouble, suffering, or responsibility]!" (AMPC).

That, my friend, describes you. As you've walked through the pages of this book, through your own pain journey, you've done so with courage and bravery, and you have made spiritual progress upon your places of pain and suffering. You are stronger for it. Your faith is more unwavering, and your focus is on the One who promises his presence amid your pain.

You can declare along with the apostle Paul, "I have fought the good fight and kept the faith." We look forward to the day when we receive the crown of righteousness because we've longed for and pursued God's presence (see 2 Tim. 4:7–8).

You may not yet be where you want to be with respect to your pain journey, but I encourage you to extend yourself grace and to celebrate each and every minute of victory. Your enemy will not have the last word because you are overcoming, and through your pain journey you have earned the credentials to link arms with other pain sufferers through the common bond you share.

My prayer is that you will chronicle, through "stones of encouragement," the journey you've taken, the lessons you've learned, and the ways God met you in your greatest need so that you'll never forget the beauty God has given you in exchange for the ashes of your pain.

You remain in my heart because of this journey we've walked together.

Hope prevails,
Dr. Michelle

Acknowledgments

The experience of writing this book was different from any other—I was more isolated because of both pain and circumstances. Yet the memories of previous contributions to my writing efforts from others, including time, encouragement, prayers, and physical resources like a loaned desk and a writing retreat, kept me going. Even in your physical absence, the previous graciousness toward my writing efforts encouraged me to forge through the crucible of pain when I was tempted on many occasions to give up.

To my fellow pain sojourner, I cannot begin to estimate the number of times I thought of you while writing this book: who you are, what you'd need, what pain you endure, or how you'd respond. You were my motivation to push through on my particularly painful days. You hold a very special place in my heart.

To my "hard-hat responders," you've come to recognize the posting of my yellow hard hat on social media as a sign that I couldn't make it without your prayer support. I read every supporting comment and offer of prayer, and I remain grateful for the strength and determination your support lends me. And a special thanks goes to Terry Palmer, who years ago suggested the hard-hat symbol to request the prayers of others to help build the "prayer wall of faith" around me. Little did I know how truly valuable that would become.

To Jessica, my Tuesday morning writing partner, our weekly sessions have been like a ray of sunshine after a week of rain. I always look forward to those times, knowing that I will force myself to rise above my pain and put my fingers to the keyboard so as not to let you down. As we often jokingly say, a few minutes of writing is better than no writing, and our times together were usually just what I needed to continue in my writing pursuits throughout the day.

Proverbs 27:17 declares that "iron sharpens iron." I'm grateful to my mastermind sisters who help sharpen my faith and my words as we lift each other up, pray for each other, cheer each other on, and encourage each other during the difficult spells.

At the onset of my formal writing career, God impressed upon me the need for a few loyal prayer warriors whom I could call, text, or DM at any hour with immediate prayer needs. You know who you are, and so does our heavenly Father. I'm grateful for your outpouring of love, sacrifice, and prayerful support, especially during the deeply pain-ridden days when I couldn't proceed in my own strength. Your ministry to me through my pain-filled cries now extends to my fellow pain sojourners who hold this book in their hands and know they aren't alone.

Thanks to my team at Revell: Vicki, Rachel, Kristin, Holly, Brianna, Olivia, and Eileen. Without you and your belief in this project, I likely would have kept my pain to myself instead of encouraging others through it.

Tawny, I'm grateful for your belief in me and in the message God placed on my heart. I hope this book makes you proud.

Cynthia, I'm grateful to God for crossing our paths, knitting our hearts together one hope-filled message at a time. I look forward to many more projects together.

Special thanks to our #HopePrevails community on Facebook for the way you've rallied around me and each other, holding dear the confidences shared there and willingly praying for and encouraging each other.

Scott, your belief in me encouraged me on the days when all I could say was, "I don't think I can." You've always believed and encouraged me that I can do whatever God has called me to, even if I needed your nudging to periodically rest and resume another day.

Blake and Bryce, thank you for loving your mom through every manuscript, even if it meant a bit of your life was revealed as well. My prayer is that one day you will be proud of the way I stewarded our family's pain for God's glory.

Jesus, you bore our pain. When I have had nowhere else to turn, you've been there. I owe you everything because you gave everything for me.

Notes

Chapter 1 Encouragement *through* Pain

1. Dr. Michelle Bengtson, *Today Is Going to Be a Good Day: 90 Promises from God to Start Your Day Off Right* (Grand Rapids: Revell, 2022).
2. *Merriam-Webster*, s.v. "encourage (*n.*)," accessed November 10, 2022, https://www.merriam-webster.com/dictionary/encourage.
3. Dr. Michelle Bengtson, *Hope Prevails: Insights from a Doctor's Personal Journey through Depression* (Grand Rapids: Revell, 2016).

Chapter 2 What Is Pain?

1. *Merriam-Webster*, s.v. "pain (*n.*)," accessed November 30, 2022, https://www.merriam-webster.com/dictionary/pain.
2. Wordnik, s.v. "suffering (*n.*)," from *The Century Dictionary*, accessed November 30, 2022, https://www.wordnik.com/words/suffering.

Chapter 3 Crawling from Moment to Moment

1. Dr. Michelle Bengtson, *Hope Prevails: Insights from a Doctor's Personal Journey through Depression* (Grand Rapids: Revell, 2016), 83.

Chapter 5 Choose Your Focus

1. Dictionary.com, s.v. "wilderness (*n.*)," accessed June 16, 2022, https://www.dictionary.com/browse/wilderness.

Chapter 7 Permission to Lament

1. Dictionary.com, s.v. "lament (*v.*)," accessed December 6, 2022, https://www.dictionary.com/browse/lament.

2. *Shivah* is defined as "a traditional seven-day period of mourning the death of a family member that is observed in Jewish homes," *Merriam-Webster*, s.v. "shivah (*n.*)," accessed December 6, 2022, https://www.merriam -webster.com/dictionary/shivah.

Chapter 11 Flip the Script on Pain

1. Bessel van der Kolk, *The Body Keeps the Score: Brain, Mind, and Body in the Healing of Trauma* (New York: Penguin Books, 2014), 21.

2. Van der Kolk, *The Body Keeps the Score*, 27.

3. Macrina Wiederkehr, *Seven Sacred Pauses: Living Mindfully Through the Hours of the Day* (Notre Dame: Sorin Books, 2008), 77.

Chapter 13 Beauty for Ashes

1. Wordnik, s.v. "compassion (*n.*)," from *The American Heritage Dictionary of the English Language*, 5th ed., accessed December 14, 2022, https://www.wordnik.com/words/compassion.

Dr. Michelle Bengtson is an international speaker, a national and international media resource on mental health, and the author of the bestselling, multi-award-winning books *Hope Prevails* and the *Hope Prevails Bible Study*. Her book *Breaking Anxiety's Grip* won the 2020 AWSA Golden Scroll Book of the Year and the 2021 Christian Literary Reader's Choice Award in four different categories. She is also the host of the award-winning podcast *Your Hope-Filled Perspective*. A board-certified clinical neuropsychologist in private practice for more than twenty years, Dr. Bengtson blogs regularly and offers a wide variety of resources on her website, DrMichelleB.com.

DrMichelleBengtson.com

Dr. Michelle Bengtson

DrMichelleBengtson

DrMBengtson

DrMichelleB

Check Out the *Your Hope-Filled Perspective* Podcast with

Dr. Michelle Bengtson

Explore More Resources from

Dr. Michelle Bengtson